The

Bible

and the

Transgender

Experience

THE BIBLE AND THE TRANSGENDER EXPERIENCE

How Scripture Supports Gender Variance

Linda Tatro Herzer

THE PILGRIM PRESS
CLEVELAND

. . .

to Gabrielle

. . .

without whose sharing and support
this book would not have come to be

. . .

and to you

if your head needs a reason to believe
what your heart already knows

. . .

The Pilgrim Press, 700 Prospect Avenue, Cleveland, Ohio 44115
thepilgrimpress.com
© 2016 by Linda Ann Herzer

Printed in the United States of America on acid-free paper.

21 22 23 24   7 6 5 4

ISBN 978-0-8298-2042-3

CONTENTS

PREFACE

In 2012 my life's journey brought me—a straight, nontransgender, middle-aged, middle-class minister—onto the staff of what was then a predominantly LGBTQI (lesbian, gay, bisexual, transgender, queer/questioning, intersex) congregation. It turns out I was an answer to the pastor's prayer that straight folks would start coming to the church so they could be more inclusive—which they now are!

It also turned out that this church was very inclusive of the transgender community. On any given Sunday, approximately 10 percent of our worshiping congregation fell somewhere under the transgender umbrella. We had trans men and trans women, cross-dressers, and those who identified as two-spirit and genderqueer. I quickly realized I needed to augment the seminary education I had received back in the 1980s to effectively minister to all my new congregants!

Consequently, I began listening to the stories of my transgender parishioners and attending conferences and support groups for gender variant individuals, that is, for those persons for whom the traditional categories "male" and "female" did not adequately define who they knew themselves to be. (I will define all these terms in chapters 1 and 2.) I read and studied and basically availed myself of any and every possible resource that would help me learn more about those who identified as gender variant. However, when I looked for books on what the Bible has to say about the transgender experience, I found very few. Consequently, I decided to write this book, based on what I have learned during these past four years.

I am deeply indebted to all the congregants and staff of that church, City of Light Atlanta, for welcoming me and freely sharing their journeys. I am especially grateful to the Rev. Dr. Paul Graetz for praying me into his congregation, nurturing my gifts, and opening many doors for me during the three years I was there.

I would also like to express deep appreciation to Rhonda Lee and all the members and significant others of Sigma Epsilon for their warm welcome and support.

My sincerest appreciation for the publishing staff at The Pilgrim Press—Tina, Julie, and Aimée—and to my wonderful copy editor, Kris. It has been a pleasure working with each of you!

Special thanks to those who have helped me with various aspects of creating this book: Gabrielle, Byron, Joanie, Darlene, Michael, Peterson, John, Larry, Dona, Bob, Sue, Cliff, Rhonda, Megan, Phoebe, Stephanie, and my daughter, Katie.

Many thanks to all my friends and family for their support and encouragement these past four years and especially to Michael, Gary, Gabrielle, Joanie, Dona, Andrea, Leslie, Sue, Cheryl, and my daughter, brother, and parents.

In the same way that it takes a community to raise a child, it has been the influence of the friends in many faith communities that has helped me grow into the person I am today. Deep gratitude to the members of the United Methodist churches in which I grew up, my Tufts Christian Fellowship friends, Asbury Theological Seminary classmates and professors, members of my first parish in upstate New York, the Atlanta breathwork community, my friends at Central Congregational UCC and Kirkwood UCC, and the women of the Harnessing Your Divine Feminine community. Blessings to all of you!

Blessings to you also, my reader, whether you are an old friend or one I have yet to meet. May God use this book to help you find the wisdom you seek—personally, professionally, and/or as a citizen of communities where transgender issues are being debated and legislated with growing frequency.

part one

LAYING THE GROUNDWORK

I

WHAT WE ARE AND ARE NOT TALKING ABOUT

LGB and TQI

I am a minister who identifies as straight and nontransgender. Four years ago I joined the staff of a church where most of our congregants identified as gay, lesbian, or transgender. As a result, I began encountering the acronym "LGBTQI" with some frequency. I learned that "LGBTQI" is an abbreviation for "lesbian, gay, bisexual, transgender, queer/questioning, and intersex." I also learned that lumping all these letters together sometimes leads to the misunderstanding that being L, G, or B is the same as being T, Q, or I. However, this is not the case. There are some very important distinctions between these terms. (If these terms are new to you, as some of them were to me, know that I will explain them in greater detail in the next chapter.)

The words "gay," "lesbian," and "bisexual" refer to one's *sexual orientation*. Sexual orientation, generally speaking, has to do with whom one is attracted to romantically. The word "transgender," broadly speaking, refers to one's *gender identity and/or one's gender expression*. Gender identity has to do with a person's internal sense of themselves, whether they know themselves to be a woman, a man, or possibly both or neither. Gender expression has to do with how people outwardly express their gender through dress, mannerisms, hairstyles, vocal inflections, and so on.

My transgender congregants helped me understand that being transgender has nothing to do with one's sexual orientation, that gender identity and sexual orientation are two totally different things. They explained it this way: Being gay is about who you go to bed *with*; being transgender is about who you go to bed *as*. Consequently, transgender individuals can be gay or straight or bisexual or any of the various sexual orientations that human beings experience.

Regarding the "Q" and the "I" in "LGBTQI," persons identifying as queer or "questioning" could be referring to their sexual orientation, their gender identity, their gender expression, and/or all three. The word "intersex" refers to one's *biology*. People who are intersex are born with genitals, internal reproductive organs, or chromosome patterns that do not fit typical definitions of male or female.[1]

Many helpful books have been written about what the Bible has to say about homosexuality, that is, about the LGB, so that is not what we will look at here. In this book, we will consider what scripture has to say about the TQI—about gender and biological variance. So let's begin!

2

CULTURAL CONTEXT

Now and Then

When I was earning my Master of Divinity degree at Asbury Theological Seminary, our professors taught us that, when it comes to understanding the Bible, "context is everything!" This meant that we were never to try to understand scripture by simply looking at an isolated verse.

I once heard a joke that illustrates this point. A person was feeling discouraged and uncertain about their future direction. They decided to look in the Bible to find guidance for their life. The Good Book fell open to Matthew 27:5, "He [Judas] went out and hanged himself." Not finding that to be very encouraging, the person decided to try again. So they put their finger down on another random page and read, "Go and do likewise" (Luke 10:37). Surprised, they tried a third time, opening to "What you are about to do, do quickly" (John 13:27). Truly, context *is* everything!

The *cultural* context of the transgender experience in America today is very different from that of biblical times. It is also important to understand that the modern context of the trans experience, which includes the very words used to describe that experience, is highly fluid, continually shifting and changing. I am about to offer some basic definitions and descriptions. However, if you are reading this book much past 2017, you may want to check a website like that of the

National Center for Transgender Equality (www.transequality.org) for more up-to-date definitions and information. Likewise, not everyone currently agrees on the definitions and usage of these terms, and usage may vary from country to country. Keeping these disclaimers in mind, let's first try to arrive at an understanding of the cultural context of gender variance in the United States today. Then we will consider the biblical context.

TRANSGENDER—AN UMBRELLA TERM AND A SPECIFIC TERM

Today the word "transgender" is commonly used as an umbrella term that includes many categories of gender variant individuals. Chances are you have seen media coverage of trans celebrities like Caitlyn Jenner, Laverne Cox, Janet Mock, Chaz Bono, and Jazz Jennings. Or perhaps you have watched television shows featuring trans characters, programs like *Glee, Orange is the New Black, Trans-Parent, Sense8,* and *The Bold and the Beautiful*, or reality shows featuring trans individuals such as *Becoming Us, I Am Cait, I Am Jazz*, and several seasons of *America's Next Top Model.* If so, you are familiar with one category of trans persons, namely, those who used to be called transsexual but are now usually just described collectively as transgender or simply "trans." (Note: The word "transgender" is an adjective, not a noun, so you would not refer to transgender persons as "transgenders.") Individually, trans people may be referred to as a "trans woman" or a "trans man," or as MTF (male to female) or FTM (female to male). These are persons whose gender identity does not match the gender they were assigned at birth.[1]

Most transgender individuals desire to live "full time" as the gender they identify as, so they dress and style their hair and present themselves accordingly, as much as they feel they can. (Lack of financial resources, state laws, or fear of losing friends, family members, church membership, and careers keep some trans people from living full time in what they know to be their true gender identity or making all the changes they might like to make.) Most transgender adults and some trans teens take, or wish to take, steps to medically alter their biology. According to these individuals' personal preferences and available resources, such steps could include taking hormones, electrolysis, and/or surgical operations. (A word about proper etiquette: Because a transgender person's gender identity is about who they know themselves to be internally, it is *never* appropriate to ask about their external anatomy or what surgeries they have had.)

I was surprised to learn that taking testosterone will drop a trans man's voice and allow him to grow facial hair. However, taking estrogen does not raise the pitch of a trans woman's voice, and, while it slightly retards facial hair growth, it does not stop it. Because of the impact of hormones on voices and hair growth, trans men are more likely to "pass" than are trans women. In fact, the first time I had a conversation with a trans man, I never even realized that the deep-voiced man with a full beard with whom I was speaking was transgender . . . until he made a reference to that fact about ten minutes into our conversation!

Trans men and trans women usually seek to change their name and the gender marker on their legal documents such as driver licenses and passports, although states have different laws governing this process. Those who are coming out as adults often find themselves in marriage and family counseling and possibly in the process of divorcing. Some marriages survive the revelation that one spouse is transgender; others do not. Teens and young adults who come out as transgender may be cut off from parental support. If they do not receive parental support, these young people often end up homeless and on the streets. Trans people who are members of faith communities often fear rejection from these communities and struggle with what it means to relate to their Higher Power as a trans person. Some ultimately leave their faith traditions while others develop an even deeper and more meaningful spiritual life. Many trans individuals struggle with employment issues, often finding themselves unemployed, underemployed, or dealing with harassment in the workplace if they are employed.[2]

The years-long process during which transgender individuals are making various social, legal, and medical changes is referred to as "transitioning." I have had the honor of becoming good friends with a trans woman in transition. When I first met Gabrielle, she had only been out for two years and had just recently made the decision to live full time as the woman she knew herself to be. During the last four years I have stood in line with her at the DMV to get a new license, nursed her through surgery, cheered when the judge pronounced her legal name change, cried with her when she struggled with family issues, and celebrated when she was honored as Atlanta's Best Trans Activist for 2015. Most importantly, I have supported Gabrielle in her journey of coming to understand that God loves her just as she is and has a wonderful purpose for her life.

CROSS-DRESSERS

I have also had the honor of attending a monthly meeting for another group of people under the transgender umbrella, a support group meeting of a chapter of Tri-Ess. Tri-Ess is an international educational, social, and support group for cross-dressers and their significant others.[3] While there are individuals who cross-dress as a fetish, that is not what members of Tri-Ess do. From these individuals and their significant others I have learned that, unlike trans men and trans women, cross-dressers *do* identify primarily with the gender they were assigned at birth, but they also need to express, experience, and spend some hours living as their "opposite" gender. What this means for these individuals is that they are comfortable living in the gender they were assigned at birth and have no desire to alter their bodies with hormones or surgeries. But now and then—and the amount of time varies from individual to individual—each of them has, not just a *desire*, but a real *need* to dress and act and be treated as a member of the opposite sex. Typically they do not cross-dress in their workplace, but many feel a need to share their identity as a cross-dresser with their family members. This often creates relational challenges, but those challenges are usually worked through and family relationships typically remain intact because cross-dressing is an occasional, not a full-time, gender expression.

Because cross-dressers rarely feel a need to share their gender expression with people other than family members, most people never know that they know cross-dressers . . . unless the cross-dresser happens to be someone's spouse or parent. Consequently, as of this writing, our culture as a whole is more aware of transgender children, teens, and adults than we are of cross-dressers.

One common misconception is that drag queens and drag kings are cross-dressers. This is usually not the case. While it is true that drag queens and kings are persons who cross-dress, they typically do it for the purpose of entertainment. Cross-dressers, on the other hand, are persons who present in the clothing of the opposite sex in order to experience their feminine or masculine essence. If cross-dressers are at a club, they are usually trying to pass, to blend in; they are typically *not* the ones up on stage!

INTERSEX PERSONS

Today in the United States there are a variety of other people who are also included under the transgender/gender variant umbrella. Intersex persons, sometimes referred to as persons with differences of sex development (DSD), are individuals born with internal and/or external sex organs and/or chromosome patterns that are different from typical males and females. Like the word "transgender," "intersex" is also an umbrella term including several dozen different types of physical conditions that are currently classified as intersex.[4] While intersex is sometimes included under the transgender umbrella, it should be noted that most intersex persons feel their gender identity *does* match the gender they were assigned at birth, thus, most intersex people *do not* identify as transgender when the term is used in its particular sense.[5] Nonetheless, because their physical beings do not match culture's expectations of typical males and females, intersex persons do experience a marginalization similar to that experienced by gender variant people. As Georgiann Davis, intersex person, professor, sociologist, and author of *Contesting Intersex: The Dubious Diagnosis,* wrote in a blog:

> I do feel that society's discriminatory view of intersex is some-thing all intersex people struggle with on a day-to-day basis. Because of narrow understandings of sex, gender, and even sexuality, intersex kids do face marginalization and ostraciza-tion from their peers, teachers, and in some cases, even their families.[6]

Thus, while most intersex persons do not identify as transgender, per se, their societal experience has many similarities to that of gender variant individuals. (See chapters 6 and 7 for further discussion of the intersex experience.)

OTHER GENDER VARIANT PERSONS

Genderqueer persons identify as neither entirely male nor entirely female, whereas bigender persons identify strongly with both genders and see themselves as both male *and* female. Calling on their own tra-ditions, some Native Americans use the term "two-spirit" for gay, les-bian, bisexual, *and* transgender persons in their cultures.[7] Likewise, there are many other terms and people under the transgender umbrella, as evidenced by the fact that in 2014 Facebook introduced fifty different terms for individuals to use to categorize their gender identity and expressions on their personal pages![8]

GENDER VARIANCE IN THE BIBLICAL CONTEXT: EUNUCHS

Needless to say, our modern cultural context is very different from the biblical context. If you are familiar with scripture, you know that nowhere in the Bible do we find the words "transgender," "cross-dresser," "intersex," "genderqueer," "bigender," or "two-spirit." Historically speaking, these are modern terms, which do not show up in our two-thousand-plus-year-old Bible. However, that does not mean there are not gender variant folks in the Bible!

In biblical times, the main group of gender variant people were eunuchs. These were men who had either been born eunuchs (Matt. 19:11–12) or who had been castrated for various reasons, often as the result of military conquest. Eunuchs were sometimes advisors and high-ranking officials in royal courts. Often they served as protectors and overseers of royal women since they were now considered "safe" to be around women because they had been surgically altered. Lacking the ability to procreate relegated eunuchs to the category of gender variant and caused them to be looked down upon in ancient Jewish culture.[9]

To understand why eunuchs were not highly esteemed back then, we need to know that in the early days of Israel's history the Jews were just a small tribe. Since they were constantly in danger of being overrun by neighboring peoples, producing children to maintain and build up the tribe was a highly valued cultural trait. Because eunuchs could not fulfill this critical gender expectation, they were definitely viewed as different, as gender variant.

So while the Bible does not specifically say anything about the categories of gender variant people that we know about in today's culture, we can look at what it says about the gender variant people of its day, the eunuchs, and see what we can learn that might be relevant in today's context.

part two

EXPLICIT VERSES AND ARGUMENTS

3

VERSES ABOUT EUNUCHS

Deuteronomy 23:1, Isaiah 56:1–7, Acts 8:26–39

In chapter 2 we noted that eunuchs were the main group of gender variant people in biblical times, at least according to the biblical record. Since procreating was so necessary for Israel's survival and thus highly valued in Jewish culture, to be castrated or to be a eunuch from birth and unable to produce heirs made one *highly* gender variant. In considering what the Scriptures have to say about eunuchs we may learn some principles relevant to gender variant people today.

DEUTERONOMY 23:1

In Deuteronomy 23:1 we find a verse prohibiting eunuchs from the assembly. Let's consider this passage in its context.

> ¹No one who has been emasculated by crushing or cutting may enter the assembly of the LORD.
>
> ²No one born of a forbidden marriage [footnote: or *one of illegitimate birth*] nor any of their descendants may enter the assembly of the LORD, not even in the tenth generation.
>
> ³No Ammonite or Moabite or any of their descendants may enter the assembly of the LORD, not even in the tenth generation. ⁴For they did not come to meet you with bread and

water on your way when you came out of Egypt, and they hired Balaam son of Beor from Pethor in Aram Naharaim to pronounce a curse on you. ⁵However, the LORD your God would not listen to Balaam but turned the curse into a blessing for you, because the LORD your God loves you. ⁶Do not seek a treaty of friendship with them as long as you live.

⁷Do not despise an Edomite, for the Edomites are related to you. Do not despise an Egyptian, because you resided as foreigners in their country. ⁸The third generation of children born to them may enter the assembly of the LORD. (Deut. 23:1–8)

The New International Version of the Bible, from which these verses are taken, introduces them with the heading "Exclusion from the Assembly" because this passage has to do with who was in and who was out—who was included and who was excluded from the "assembly," the term for the sacred gathering of God's people in that day, similar to the gathering of Christians for worship in churches today. During Israel's early history, eunuchs and "foreigners" (all people who were not Israelites) were on the "excluded" list.

Was that prohibition binding for all time? No. Within scripture itself we see the prohibition regarding eunuchs and foreigners change over time.

ISAIAH 56:1–7

In Isaiah 56 the prophet writes about how God relates to *all* those whose actions show that they are following God, including eunuchs and foreigners, the very people who were excluded from the Lord's assembly in Deuteronomy 23.

¹This is what the LORD says: "Maintain justice and do what is right, for my salvation is close at hand and my righteousness will soon be revealed. ²Blessed is the one who does this—the person who holds it fast, who keeps the Sabbath without desecrating it, and keeps their hands from doing any evil."

³Let no foreigner who is bound to the LORD say, "The LORD will surely exclude me from his people." And let no eunuch complain, "I am only a dry tree."

⁴For this is what the LORD says: "To the eunuchs who keep my Sabbaths, who choose what pleases me and hold fast to my covenant—⁵to them I will give within my temples and its walls a memorial and a name better than sons and daughters; I will give them an everlasting name that will endure forever.

⁶And foreigners who bind themselves to the LORD to minister to him, to love the name of the LORD, and to be his servants, all who keep the Sabbath without desecrating it and who hold fast to my covenant—⁷these I will bring to my holy mountain and give them joy in my house of prayer. Their burnt offerings and sacrifices will be accepted on my altar; for my house will be called a house of prayer for all nations. (Isa. 56:1–7)

Here the prophet Isaiah foretells a time when God will lift the prohibitions on those who were formerly outsiders and outcasts; all gender variant eunuchs and foreigners who love God will be honored and included in the assembly.

ACTS 8:26–39

Moving forward in Jewish history, we see this inclusion come to pass in the New Testament as the good news about Jesus begins to spread. Acts 8:26–39 tells the story of Philip and the Ethiopian eunuch.

²⁶Now an angel of the Lord said to Philip, "Go south to the road—the desert road—that goes down from Jerusalem to Gaza." ²⁷So he started out, and on his way he met an Ethiopian eunuch, an important official in charge of all the treasury of the Kandake (which means "queen of the Ethiopians"). This man had gone to Jerusalem to worship,

²⁸and on his way home was sitting in his chariot reading the Book of Isaiah the prophet. ²⁹The Spirit told Philip, "Go to that chariot and stay near it."

³⁰Then Philip ran up to the chariot and heard the man reading Isaiah the prophet. "Do you understand what you are reading?" Philip asked.

³¹"How can I," he said, "unless someone explains it to me?" So he invited Philip to come up and sit with him.

³²This is the passage of Scripture the eunuch was reading:
> "He was led like a sheep to the slaughter,
>   and as a lamb before its shearer is silent,
>   so he did not open his mouth.

³³In his humiliation he was deprived of justice.
>   Who can speak of his descendants?
>   For his life was taken from the earth."

³⁴The eunuch asked Philip, "Tell me, please, who is the prophet talking about, himself or someone else?" ³⁵Then Philip began with that very passage of Scripture and told him the good news about Jesus. (Acts 8:26–35)

It is important to note that this passage of scripture the eunuch is reading is the 53rd chapter of Isaiah, commonly known as the "Suffering Servant" passage because it foretells what happens during Jesus's trial and crucifixion. I think it is also important to note that this Suffering Servant passage that the eunuch is reading occurs just three chapters before the preceding passage from Isaiah 56, where Isaiah foretold God's acceptance of eunuchs. Since Acts 8:35 says that Philip *began* with that Suffering Servant passage of scripture from Isaiah 53, perhaps Philip *ended up* three chapters over, in Isaiah 56, telling the Ethiopian eunuch how Jesus demonstrated this radical welcome of eunuchs and foreigners that Isaiah foretold. It seems likely that Philip continued on to chapter 56 because of what happens next.

> ³⁶As they traveled along the road, they came to some water and the eunuch said, "Look, here is water. What can stand in the way of my being baptized?" (Acts 8:36)

The way the eunuch asks that question—"What can stand in the way of my being baptized?"—implies that this person is used to having people and things stand in the way of his full acceptance in society. The eunuch's boldness in asking that question suggests that whatever Philip shared gave him the courage to believe that he, too, was loved and welcomed and accepted by God. Here's how the story ends.

> ³⁸And he gave orders to stop the chariot. Then both Philip and the eunuch went down into the water and Philip baptized him. ³⁹When they came up out of the water, the Spirit of the Lord suddenly took Philip away, and the eunuch did not see him again, but went on his way rejoicing. (Acts 8:38–39)

Here in the book of Acts, during the early days of the Christian Church, God's desire to include eunuchs and foreigners in the assembly, foretold in Isaiah 56, comes to pass. A gender variant, probably black, African eunuch is baptized into the family of God!

THE SHIFT FROM EXCLUSION TO INCLUSION

Thus, the Bible clearly shows a change in attitude towards the inclusion of eunuchs in God's assembly . . . from Deuteronomic prohibition, to Isaiah's prophesy of inclusion, to the baptism of the Ethiopian eunuch recounted in the book of Acts. Such a movement from exclusion to inclusion mirrors the entire contextual trajectory of the Scriptures in general.

Exclusions concerning Gentiles are another case in point. Much to the surprise of Jesus' first Jewish followers, God breaks the barriers between Jews and Gentiles by baptizing Gentiles with the Holy Spirit, thus signifying God's acceptance of them (Acts 10, 11, and 15). Likewise, one of the main reasons Jesus was crucified was because he chose to include people on the grounds of love instead of excluding them on the basis of the Old Testament law.

The fact that the Bible itself shows a historical movement and shift in the Israelites' understanding of how God would have them relate to the gender variant people of their day suggests that God may also have an accepting, affirming, and inclusive attitude towards the gender variant people of our day. If that is God's attitude, then gender variant people everywhere should rejoice, and those of us who profess to be Christ's followers should exhibit the same acceptance, affirmation, and inclusion of gender nonconforming individuals that the Bible reveals.

WHY WERE THERE EXCLUSIVE LAWS IN THE FIRST PLACE?

This historical movement from exclusion to inclusion, which is prevalent in the Scriptures, causes me to wonder: "What was the basis for all those exclusions in the first place? Why were passages like Deuteronomy 23:1 ever even written?" In case you may also wonder about this, I offer my thoughts on what I have come to understand about this.

The biblical stories themselves testify that the Israelites were just one small tribe struggling for survival among other tribes, some of them much larger, that were fighting for the same territory they wanted to occupy. This means that the laws in Deuteronomy were given to people who struggled with the fear of being wiped out by their neighbors.

Those of us who have lived through or studied recent American history are familiar with the kind of exclusionary mentality that such fears create. Not so many years ago, when Americans felt threatened after the attack on Pearl Harbor, it became national policy to exclude Japanese Americans. Consequently, thousands of these innocent, loyal U.S. citizens were rounded up and sent to internment camps. Even more recently, after 9/11, we heard many stories of Middle Eastern–looking individuals who experienced harassment and detainment as a result of the fear that gripped our country. Likewise, we may have heard stories of first, second, and even third generation immigrant parents wanting their children to "marry their own kind" to help preserve their culture so it does not get lost in American culture, that is, become blended in with the "larger tribe." Such thinking is humorously portrayed in the movies *My Big Fat Greek Wedding*, 1 and 2! These are contemporary examples of exclusionary actions that have resulted from threats to national security and cultural survival.

These examples help me understand the thinking that may have given rise to the exclusionary laws found in Deuteronomy and also in Leviticus. (See the next chapter for more about this.) Obviously the writers of the Old Testament believed they were writing God's words to them and God's will for them. Yet the New Testament reveals through Jesus, God's Word made flesh, through the baptism of the Ethiopian eunuch, and through the outpouring of the Holy Spirit on Gentiles that inclusion, not exclusion, is God's will. Consequently, these ancient Israelites may have been hearing God's word to them through the lens of their own fears, so they wrote that it was God's will that they exclude others . . . a perspective God later corrected through Isaiah, Jesus, and the Acts of the Holy Spirit.

This is not to say that the Bible is not God's Word, that it is merely the words of people. No. I suggest this perspective because the Bible itself testifies that God can only give God's people what they are able to accept. This principle is revealed in 1 Samuel 8 when God tells Samuel that God's intent was to be Israel's one and only king. However, because Israel rejected Yahweh and served other gods, Yahweh *allowed* them to have a human king. In the same way, perhaps God was aware that, because of their fears and insecurities, the Israelites would only be able to accept exclusionary, "circle the wagons," "take care of me and mine" rules and regulations, so God allowed that, as a less than best option. Then, in the fullness of time, God revealed God's true intent, through Isaiah and through the Word made flesh: God's intention to include all people in God's assembly, to include foreigners and eunuchs, the Gentiles, and the gender variant.

This is just one explanation for why we see in scripture a movement from the exclusion of eunuchs in God's assembly to the inclusion of eunuchs in the family of God. In the next chapter I will suggest another possible reason for this change. While these speculations have value, the most important thing for us to keep in mind is that a significant change *did* occur; the Ethiopian eunuch, a member of the gender variant, foreign outcasts described in the Old Testament, was welcomed as a baptized follower of Christ in the New Testament.

4

LEVITICUS 21 AND HOLINESS

In the previous chapter we began a consideration of explanations for why we find within the Bible itself a movement from excluding to including eunuchs. In Leviticus 21 we find another exclusionary passage and more clues as to the reasons behind such exclusions.

As you may know, the Levites were the one tribe out of the twelve tribes of Israel that served God as priests. The title of this biblical book, Leviticus, literally means "about the Levites" and the book details the rules and regulations they were to follow regarding worship and making sacrifices. In my NIV Bible, the "Introduction to Leviticus" says, "Although many of the rules were given only for the Levites, the purpose of all the laws that were given was to help the Israelites worship and live as God's holy people. A key statement for the entire book is 'Be holy, because I am holy'" (Lev. 11:44, 45).[1]

In the twenty-first chapter of Leviticus we find examples of some of these laws. Here I include much of this chapter so we will have a feel for the context of verse 20, a verse that might be used to exclude trans women who have had genital surgery or who take hormones from ordination, if taken out of context and misunderstood.

[1]The LORD said to Moses, "Speak to the priests, the sons of Aaron, and say to them: 'A priest must not make himself ceremonially

unclean for any of his people who die, ²except for a close relative, such as his mother or father, his son or daughter, his brother. . . .

⁵"Priests must not shave their heads or shave off the edges of their beards or cut their bodies. ⁶They must be holy to their God and must not profane the name of their God. Because they present the food offerings to the LORD, the food of their God, they are to be holy.

⁷"They must not marry women defiled by prostitution or divorced from their husbands, because priests are holy to their God. ⁸Regard them as holy, because they offer up the food of your God. Consider them holy, because I the LORD am holy— I who make you holy.

⁹"If a priest's daughter defiles herself by becoming a prostitute, she disgraces her father; she must be burned in the fire. . . .'"

¹⁶The LORD said to Moses, ¹⁷"Say to Aaron: 'For the generations to come none of your descendants who has a defect may come near to offer the food of his God. ¹⁸No man who has any defect may come near: no man who is blind or lame, disfigured or deformed; ¹⁹no man with a crippled foot or hand, ²⁰or who is a hunchback or a dwarf, or who has any eye defect, or who has festering or running sores or damaged testicles. ²¹No descendant of Aaron the priest who has any defect is to come near to present the food offerings to the LORD. He has a defect; he must not come near to offer the food of his God. ²²He may eat the most holy food of his God, as well as the holy food; ²³yet because of his defect, he must not go near the curtain or approach the altar, and so desecrate my sanctuary. I am the LORD, who makes them holy.'" (Lev. 21: 1–23)

Such rules and regulations sound harsh and insensitive, even prejudicial to our twenty-first-century ears. Imagine telling someone seeking ordination they cannot be ordained because they have an eye defect requiring them to wear contacts or glasses, or because they suffer from lameness caused by severe arthritis! Yet this was the ancient Israelites' experience of what it took for God's priests to be holy.

CHRIST FULFILLED THE REQUIREMENTS OF THE LAW

In the same way the church no longer uses this passage to bar very short people, people who are blind or who wear corrective lenses, or people who have arthritis from ordination, this passage should also not be used to bar medically transitioned trans women from ordination. The reason the church no longer uses this passage as part of its requirements for ordination is because the New Testament reveals that, through Christ, the requirements of the Old Testament law have been fulfilled (see Acts 15, Galatians 3, Hebrews 8–10). Consequently, Christians no longer observe all the requirements of Old Testament Law, which is why denominations now have no qualms about ordaining people who wear glasses, or have arthritis, or who use a wheelchair to get around. A growing number of denominations also have transgender individuals among their ranks of ordained clergy, including the United Church of Christ, Metropolitan Community Churches, the Episcopal Church, the United Methodist Church, the Evangelical Lutheran Church in America, the Presbyterian Church (USA), and the American Baptist Convention.[2]

A DEEPER UNDERSTANDING OF PURITY AND HOLINESS

Now let us return to the question "Why do we find all these exclusionary rules and regulations in the Old Testament?" In the previous chapter I suggest that one possible explanation for this is that, due to the ancient Israelites' fears for their national security and their cultural survival, they may have only been able to hear the kind of rules that they thought would keep them safe—rules that excluded anyone who was not just like them. However, as time went by, God showed them "the most excellent way" (1 Cor. 12:31).

Within the Bible itself we likewise see God reveal "the most excellent way" in regards to what it means to be holy. The laws in Leviticus suggest that God maintained God's holiness by remaining separate from anything that might "contaminate" God's purity. Consequently, in order to be like the God they served, the Israelites also had to set themselves apart from anything impure, anything different, anything that might contaminate them. Examples from the Leviticus 21 passage of contaminants included:

- Attending a funeral (being in the presence of a dead person)
- Shaving one's head
- Marrying a divorced woman
- Any sort of physical defect

However, when Jesus came, he taught and modeled a deeper, more profound way of understanding holiness. Jesus taught that it is not the things that people come in contact with on the outside that defile them and make them unclean or unholy, but the thoughts and actions that arise from inside them.

> [1]Then some Pharisees and teachers of the law came to Jesus from Jerusalem and asked, [2]"Why do your disciples break the tradition of the elders? They don't wash their hands before they eat!"
>
> [10]. . . Jesus called the crowd to him and said, "Listen and understand. [11]What goes into someone's mouth does not defile them, but what comes out of their mouth, that is what defiles them." . . . [17]"Don't you see that whatever enters the mouth goes into the stomach and then out of the body? [18]But the things that come out of a person's mouth come from the heart, and these defile them. [19]For out of the heart come evil thoughts—murder, adultery, sexual immorality, theft, false testimony, slander. [20]These are what defile a person; but eating with unwashed hands does not defile them." (Matt. 15:1–20)

Likewise Jesus taught and demonstrated that, in spite of what it says in Leviticus 21, people with physical defects should not be considered impure, unholy, or sinful just because of their physical realities. This difference between what Jesus believed regarding holiness and the prevailing beliefs of his day are clearly portrayed in the ninth chapter of John's Gospel.

> [1]As (Jesus) went along, he saw a man blind from birth. [2]His disciples asked him, "Rabbi, who sinned, this man or his parents, that he was born blind?"
>
> [3]"Neither this man nor his parents sinned," said Jesus, "but this happened so that the works of God might be displayed in him. [4]As long as it is day, we must do the works of him who sent me. Night is coming, when no one can work. [5]While I am in the world, I am the light of the world."
>
> [6]After saying this, he spit on the ground, made some mud with the saliva, and put it on the man's eyes. [7]"Go," he told him, "wash in the Pool of Siloam" (this word means "Sent"). So the man went and washed, and came home seeing.

Christ demonstrated this new teaching, this deeper understanding of holiness in every aspect of his life. Much to the disapproval of the religious leaders of his day, Jesus even ate with "sinners and outcasts"—those considered to be impure according to the holiness teachings found in Leviticus!

Thus, within Jesus' life and teachings we see the unfolding of a deeper understanding of what it means to be holy, just as we saw, in the previous chapter, a development in the Israelites' understanding of God's inclusive nature. Consequently, we see that these verses that were once used to exclude eunuchs from God's assembly and people with crushed testicles from God's service can no longer be used in that way today. Indeed, the ongoing revelation of what it means to be holy is good news for the arthritic, the visually challenged, the vertically challenged—and for medically transitioned trans women seeking ordination or wanting to keep their ordination, as well.

5

DEUTERONOMY 22:5

Cross-Dressing to Express One's Truth or to Do Harm?

Whven I was a student at Asbury Theological Seminary, my professors taught us that a responsible interpretation of scripture required several things. First, it was important to know the actual meanings of the words we were reading, to understand what they meant in their original Greek (New Testament) or Hebrew (Old Testament). We were also taught that the best way to know the meaning of a specific word was to compare it to other places in scripture where that word was found. Once we had an understanding of the individual words in a verse, then we were to look at the story or passage in which that verse was found to be sure we were interpreting it in its proper context. (Remember the perils of the person in the joke from chapter 2 who went looking for guidance for their life and landed randomly on the verses "He went out and hung himself," "Go and do likewise," and "What you are about to do, do quickly"!) Finally, after looking at a verse in its immediate context we were to consider it in the context of the message of the whole Bible. You will recall from our discussion of eunuchs in chapter 3 and our consideration of a priest's physical defects in chapter 4 that considering a verse in the context of the message of the entire Bible can help us understand whether a prohibition was meant for God's people only in that particular time or for all time.

INTERPRETATIONS BASED ON THE MEANING OF WORDS AND IMMEDIATE CONTEXT

When attempting to come to a responsible understanding of Deuteronomy 22:5, another one of the biblical passages that appears to explicitly relate to gender variance, it is important to use all of the preceding guidelines. The passage forming the immediate context of this verse is Deuteronomy 22:1–22.

> ¹If you see your fellow Israelite's ox or sheep straying, do not ignore it but be sure to take it back to its owner. ²If they do not live near you or if you do not know who owns it, take it home with you and keep it until they come looking for it. Then give it back. ³Do the same if you find their donkey or cloak or anything else they have lost. Do not ignore it.
>
> ⁴If you see your fellow Israelite's donkey or ox fallen on the road, do not ignore it. Help the owner get it to its feet.
>
> ⁵A woman must not wear men's clothing, nor a man wear women's clothing, for the LORD your God detests anyone who does this.
>
> ⁶If you come across a bird's nest beside the road, either in a tree or on the ground, and the mother is sitting on the young or on the eggs, do not take the mother with the young. ⁷You may take the young, but be sure to let the mother go, so that it may go well with you and you may have a long life.
>
> ⁸When you build a new house, make a parapet around your roof so that you may not bring the guilt of bloodshed on your house if someone falls from the roof.
>
> ⁹Do not plant two kinds of seed in your vineyard; if you do, not only the crops you plant but also the fruit of the vineyard will be defiled.

¹⁰Do not plow with an ox and a donkey yoked together.

¹¹Do not wear clothes of wool and linen woven together.

¹²Make tassels on the four corners of the cloak you wear.

¹³If a man takes a wife and, after sleeping with her, dislikes her ¹⁴and slanders her and gives her a bad name, saying, "I married this woman, but when I approached her, I did not find proof of her virginity," ¹⁵then the young woman's father and mother shall bring to the town elders at the gate proof that she was a virgin. ¹⁶Her father will say to the elders, "I gave my daughter in marriage to this man, but he dislikes her. ¹⁷Now he has slandered her and said, 'I did not find your daughter to be a virgin.' But here is the proof of my daughter's virginity." Then her parents shall display the cloth before the elders of the town, ¹⁸and the elders shall take the man and punish him. ¹⁹They shall fine him a hundred shekels of silver and give them to the young woman's father, because this man has given an Israelite virgin a bad name. She shall continue to be his wife; he must not divorce her as long as he lives.

²⁰If, however, the charge is true and no proof of the young woman's virginity can be found, ²¹she shall be brought to the door of her father's house and there the men of her town shall stone her to death. She has done an outrageous thing in Israel by being promiscuous while still in her father's house. You must purge the evil from among you.

²²If a man is found sleeping with another man's wife, both the man who slept with her and the woman must die. You must purge the evil from Israel.

Regarding the specific meanings of some of the key words in Deuteronomy 22:5 Theresa Scott writes on her website, Theresa's Place-E,

The word in this passage that is translated here as "clothing" is:

keli OT:3627: used variously in the Bible to mean "vessel; receptacle; stuff; clothing; utensil; tool; instrument; ornament or jewelry; armor or weapon; male sex organ."

Keli appears about 320 times in the Bible and is only translated as clothing in this one passage, and there is no surrounding context which would indicate whether "clothing" is the correct translation . . .

The word translated as "man" in Deuteronomy 22:5 is:

geber OT:1396: properly, a valiant man or warrior; generally, a person simply.

With these definitions in mind, alternative translations abound. For example, one more consistent with other usage of these words might be:

"A woman shall not wear the armor of a warrior, nor shall a warrior disguise himself as a woman, for whoever does these things is an abomination to the LORD your God." (speculative Deut 22:5)[1]

Keeping this possible translation in mind, let us now consider the context of this passage.

Deuteronomy 22:5 is surrounded by verses of instructions designed to keep us from damaging our relationships with others. In the verses immediately preceding this verse we learn that we are obligated to return lost objects and help lift up our neighbor's ox if it has fallen in the road. In the verses following verse 5, we are taught proper relations to birds on their nests and given instructions on how to build our homes to keep our guests safe. Given that the context of this passage is instructions about not damaging relations between beings, we have to ask ourselves, "In what sorts of situations might dressing in the clothes or armament of the opposite gender negatively impact our relationships with others or with God, to the point that God would detest us?"

The Rev. Dr. Justin Tanis, author of *Trans-Gendered: Theology, Ministry, and Communities of Faith*, suggests several answers to this question.[2] Back in Old Testament times, dressing in clothes of the opposite gender could negatively impact one's relationship with God because, in those days, men and women often cross-dressed in practicing their worship of foreign Gods. For the Jews, worshiping other gods was like a slap in the face to their God, Yahweh. We have only to remember how angry Yahweh was with the Israelites when Moses came down from Mount Sinai and found them worshiping the golden calf (Exodus 32) to know that cross-dressing to worship foreign gods would result in God detesting God's people.

Meanwhile, cross-dressing could damage relationships with others if the person was doing it to deceive. For example, Tanis suggested that women might cross-dress to gain forbidden access to men's space. One such example of space forbidden to women was the military, and even as recently as the American Civil War there are accounts of women disguising themselves as men to fight in the army or to serve as spies. This interpretation is consistent with the literal meanings and common usage of the words *keli* (armor) and *geber* (warrior). Likewise, back in Old Testament times, women might disguise themselves in male clothes to gain access to male-only sections of the temple, similar to what Barbara Streisand did in the movie *Yentl*. Meanwhile, relations could be damaged if men disguised themselves to gain forbidden access to women's private space, especially if these men intended to do harm to women. Or men might disguise themselves as women to avoid conscription into the army. In the old TV series, *M★A★S★H*, the character of Klinger tried to use this same tactic to get *out* of the army. Again, seeing this as a prohibition against cross-dressing that relates to military service is consistent with the common usage of these Hebrew words. Thus we have seen a variety of ways in which cross-dressing, back then, could damage relations with God and others—if it was used in the worship of other gods or in order to deceive others.

In an online sermon, Rabbi Lisa Edwards focuses on another significant aspect of the context in which Deuteronomy 22:5 is situated. Rabbi Edwards notes that the phrase "do not ignore it" appears three times in these verses. Do not ignore someone's animal that has strayed. Do not ignore something you find that your neighbor has lost. Do not ignore your neighbor struggling to raise their fallen ox. She points out that the literal translation of this phrase, "Do not ignore it," is "Do not hide yourself." And while "Do not ignore it" is a nice interpretation, she suggests that it is not quite the same as "Do not hide yourself." Rabbi Edwards writes:

> "Hiding yourself is different from ignoring something or being indifferent to someone else's plight. . . . Hiding yourself is not only about shirking responsibility—it's about closeting yourself. It's about hoping no one will see you, maybe it's about hoping you won't notice yourself—won't notice who you really are. . . . Perhaps this verse (when read in its fullest context) is about not hiding yourself behind clothes that do not belong to you, that do not show who you are, that do not allow you to feel like yourself when you are wearing them."[3]

Thus, a careful consideration of the immediate context suggests that what God was telling people to do in Deuteronomy 22:5 was to *not* dress in a way that would hide their true identity and deceive others in a harmful way. Knowing that this is the intent of this verse helps us understand why there are no objections at Halloween when people dress in the clothing of the opposite gender because everyone understands that the cross-dressing is being done with no intention to harm others. It also explains why, back in Shakespeare's day, there were no objections when men dressed in women's clothes to portray female characters on the stage because the culture of that time did not yet allow women to be actors. Likewise today, when gender variant people dress in clothes that do not match the gender they were assigned at birth, there should be no objections based on this biblical passage, since they are not dressing to hide themselves so they can harm others. In fact, just the opposite is true! Gender variant individuals carefully choose their clothing so as to *not* hide themselves; so people *can* know and interact with them according to their truth.

Therefore, understood in its immediate context, this verse that appears to be a law against cross-dressing actually becomes an exhortation to modern-day gender variant individuals not to hide themselves, but to dress in the clothes that truly reflect their internal sense of themselves! This surprising perspective, which arises from a careful consideration of the context of this passage, is a perfect example of why my seminary professors told us over and over again, "Context is everything. Context is *everything*!!"

When considering context, we should also note that some commentators[4] have focused on the verses that appear several verses beyond this passage:

5A woman must not wear men's clothing, nor a man wear women's clothing, for the LORD your God detests anyone who does this.

6If you come across a bird's nest beside the road, either in a tree or on the ground, and the mother is sitting on the young or on the eggs, do not take the mother with the young. 7You may take the young, but be sure to let the mother go, so that it may go well with you and you may have a long life.

8When you build a new house, make a parapet around your roof so that you may not bring the guilt of bloodshed on your house if someone falls from the roof.

9Do not plant two kinds of seed in your vineyard; if you do, not only the crops you plant but also the fruit of the vineyard will be defiled.

[10]Do not plow with an ox and a donkey yoked together.

[11]Do not wear clothes of wool and linen woven together.

[12]Make tassels on the four corners of the cloak you wear."

Commentators who have focused on verses 9–11, which have the common theme of prohibiting the blending of two similar but distinct things, have interpreted Deuteronomy 22:5 to be a prohibition against blurring what they believe to be the God-created distinctions between male and female. These commentators argue that verses 9–11 about blurring distinctions are the context in which we should understand verse 5. The problem I see with that line of thinking is that the verse about what men and women should and should not wear is separated from verses 9–11 by three other verses—verses 6–7, giving directions on what to do when one comes across a mother bird on its nest, and verse 8, about building railings on the roofs of our homes so our guests won't fall and hurt themselves. Since verse 5 is separated from the verses about not blending things of a distinct nature by two other verses that have nothing to do with blurring distinctions, it seems the most responsible conclusion to draw is that the actual context of verse 5 is the verses it is immediately adjacent to, verses 1–8, which have to do with not harming our relations with others, as previously discussed.

In summary, the meaning of the Hebrew words in Deuteronomy 22:5 and the context of this verse suggest several possible interpretations, all of which have been put forth by various commentators throughout history. (For quotes regarding this passage from more than forty Jewish and Christian commentators, see Sandra Stewart's The Gender Tree website.[5])

1. The interpretation that is *least consistent* with the traditional use of the words *keli* (often meaning "armor," translated only in this instance as "clothing") and *geber* (warrior or person) is that this is a prohibition against cross-dressing as we understand it today. While this interpretation could be strengthened by

the observation that there are verses within the same chapter about not mixing things that are different, the fact that verse 5 is separated from these verses by two other totally unrelated admonitions suggests that this passage is *not* related to the instructions about the blending of distinct things.

2. An interpretation that is more consistent with the common use of the words *keli* and *geber* is that men and women should not dress like the opposite gender in order to deceive others, in order to gain access to spaces traditionally forbidden to persons of their gender.

3. Such an interpretation is also consistent with the literal meaning "do not hide yourself," the admonition found in the verses immediately preceding verse 5. In other words, do dress according to your true identity so as not to harm others. And that is exactly what gender variant people of today understand themselves to be doing; they are dressing in such a way that does not hide themselves, but presents their true gender to others. They dress in ways that helps people know them for who they understand themselves to be.

4. Understood in the cultural context of when this was written, it is also a definite possibility that this passage was addressing the practice of dressing in clothes of the opposite gender in order to serve in the temples of other gods, a practice that God would certainly detest and that would harm one's relationship with God.

A PROHIBITION JUST FOR THEN OR FOREVER?

Even though understanding this passage as a prohibition against cross-dressing as it is practiced by gender variant people today seems like the least responsible interpretation of this verse, for a moment let's just entertain the possibility that this *might* have been the intent of Deuteronomy 22:5. Then we must still apply the third guideline for responsible scriptural interpretation taught by my seminary professors; we must consider the passage in the context of the entire Bible. This brings us to the question, "Is verse 5 a prohibition for all time, or just for the people in that particular historical context?"

As we previously noted in chapter 4, Christians believe that Jesus fulfilled the requirements of the Old Testament law; therefore, we are no longer obligated to observe all the rules and regulations found there. That is why Christians no longer ban people with physical "defects" from ordination (chapter 4) nor observe all the other admonitions in Deuteronomy 22. We do not build railings on the roofs of our homes (v. 8) nor feel obligated to wear tassels on the four corners of our cloaks (v. 12). We freely plant a variety of seeds in our gardens (v. 9) and wear clothes of blended materials (v. 11). Regarding other regulations from Deuteronomy 22, we no longer follow the dictates in verses 20–21, to stone to death a woman who marries who cannot prove her virginity, nor do we observe the command in verse 22, to kill every man and woman caught in adultery. (Jesus did not observe this command either, according to John 8:1–11.) Consequently, if we are responsibly consistent with our interpretation of scripture, we must conclude that even if cross-dressing as it occurs today was being prohibited in Deuteronomy 22:5, it was *not* a requirement for all time. Just like all the other laws in that chapter, it was only a law for that particular era.

While this is good news for gender variant individuals today, I would just like to reiterate that, personally, I do not believe that Deuteronomy 22:5 is a verse about cross-dressing as gender variant people do in the modern era. Our careful consideration of the meanings and use of the specific words in Hebrew and the context of this verse within this chapter and the culture of its day strongly indicates that what is being addressed here is dressing in order to hide oneself and so deceive others in ways that would be harmful to relationships and/or dressing in crossgender ways in order to participate in pagan worship. Since gender variant people today are cross-dressing in order *to* express their true selves, in order to *not* deceive others and so harm relationships, I believe this verse is actually an affirmation to gender variant people to dress in the clothing that best expresses their true gender identity.

· · ·

We have considered these explicit verses, mainly from the Old Testament, that people cite in relation to the transgender experience.

- Deuteronomy 23:1, Isaiah 56:1–5 and Acts 8:26–39 regarding eunuchs
- Leviticus 21:20 regarding the physical defects of priests
- Deuteronomy 22:5 regarding cross-dressing to worship foreign gods or to hide one's true identity in order to do harm

Let us now turn our attention to the Gospels to see what Jesus had to say about gender variance.

6

MATTHEW 19:11-12 AND WHAT JESUS HAD TO SAY ABOUT GENDER VARIANCE

One evening I was attending the transgender support group offered by the church where I had recently started working. The seminarian who served as the group's chaplain had been explaining to us that eunuchs were the main category of gender variant individuals in the Bible. Then she said something that took me totally by surprise: "Now let's look at what Jesus had to say about eunuchs." I distinctly remember thinking, "W-h-a-t??? I've read *all* the gospels *many, many* times, and I don't ever remember Jesus saying anything about eunuchs!" But Jesus did . . . right there in the gospel of Matthew, chapter 19.

> Some Pharisees came to him to test him. They asked, "Is it lawful for a man to divorce his wife for any and every reason?"
>
> [4]"Haven't you read," he replied, "that at the beginning the Creator 'made them male and female,' [5]and said, 'For this reason a man will leave his father and mother and be united to his wife, and the two will become one flesh'? [6]So they are no longer two, but one flesh. Therefore what God has joined together, let no one separate."

7"Why then," they asked, "did Moses command that a man give his wife a certificate of divorce and send her away?"

8Jesus replied, "Moses permitted you to divorce your wives because your hearts were hard. But it was not this way from the beginning. 9I tell you that anyone who divorces his wife, except for sexual immorality, and marries another woman commits adultery."

10The disciples said to him, "If this is the situation between a husband and wife, it is better not to marry."

11Jesus replied, "Not everyone can accept this word, but only those to whom it has been given. 12For there are eunuchs who were born that way, and there are eunuchs who have been made eunuchs by others—and there are those who choose to live like eunuchs for the sake of the kingdom of heaven. The one who can accept this should accept it." (Matt. 19:3–12)

The context in which Jesus makes these statements about eunuchs is a discussion about marriage and divorce. This suggests that the gender variance Jesus is referring to here is the gender nonconforming act of not marrying. As you may recall from our discussion in chapter 3, marriage and procreation were highly valued cultural traits and were expected of all Jewish people. The ancient Israelites saw marriage and procreation as a means of growing their small tribe in order to protect themselves from attacks from hostile tribes and empires. This thought persisted in Jesus' day, especially seeing as the Israelites were under the dominion of the Roman Empire at that time.

Consequently, in order to understand this verse about someone being born a eunuch we must ask ourselves, "Why wouldn't some-one—from birth—not want to, or not be able to, get married so they could procreate and have legitimate heirs . . . especially in a culture where having children was a sign of God's blessing and the means by which family inheritances were passed down?" Perhaps the most obvious answer, from our twenty-first-century perspective, is because they are gay, so *from birth* they have no interest in heterosexual marriage. Another possible answer is that they were born transgender, so they have no interest in carrying out the roles and expectations typically assigned to someone with their genitals. A third possibility is that they might be intersex, persons who may have thought, because of the emphasis placed on procreation in Jesus' day, that they should not marry if their genitals, and thus perhaps their reproductive capabilities, were not typically male or female. (Fortunately, people today are realizing that being intersex is not a deterrent to being happily married, although some intersex people and their parents have worried that it might be a deterrent until they learned of the many intersex persons who are in fulfilling relationships.[1] (See more about intersex persons in chapter 7.)

I do not believe we can say, definitively, which of these three reasons—being gay, being transgender, or being intersex—Jesus was referencing when he said that some are "born eunuchs." Of course, he may have been referencing "all of the above"! Some take a literal interpretive approach and suggest that because "eunuch" literally refers to one who has been castrated, then what Jesus is referring to here is a man with an atypical reproductive organ, which would include men who were castrated and those individuals who were born intersex. However, the fact that Jesus also says in this passage, "and there are those who choose to live like eunuchs for the sake of the kingdom of heaven," suggests that he is not only speaking about literal eunuchs, but about figurative eunuchs as well, eunuchs who chose to follow a higher calling than their society's expectations of heterosexual marriage and procreation.

As I previously stated, it is hard to know definitively whether or not Jesus intended to include in this passage people who would be defined today as gay or transgender. Nevertheless, the very fact that he even mentions that the gender variant people of his day are gender variant for a variety of reasons is highly significant. Firstly, it suggests that Jesus must have known at least one eunuch who was born that way; he must have known at least one person who was born intersex or perhaps gay or transgender. He also must have known those, like himself, who chose a gender variant path for the sake of a higher calling. (Most scholars agree that Jesus was not married, which would make him a gender variant individual in his society.)

Secondly, the context in which these words of Jesus appear suggests that, along with the genders of male and female, Jesus also recognized that there actually *is* gender variance. This is highly significant because some Christians take Matthew 19:4 out of context and use this verse to argue that Jesus believed that, from the beginning, God has created only males and females.[2]

> "Haven't you read," he [Jesus] replied, "that at the beginning the Creator 'made them male and female' . . . ?" (Matt. 19:4)

Granted, if this was all that Jesus had said regarding gender in this passage, then it might indicate that Jesus believed that God created only male and female. However, this is not all that Jesus said about gender in Matthew 19. This is not just a chapter about male, female, divorce, and marriage. In the full context of this conversation Jesus discusses marriage, divorce, male, female, *and* eunuchs. The fact that Jesus included the one thing the Gospels report him saying about gender variance in the very same conversation in which he quotes the verse about God creating humans male and female (Gen. 1:27) indicates that Jesus was well aware that there were more than just two ways to live out one's gender—that male and female were not the only two realities.

Let me repeat that.

Jesus was well aware that there were more than just two ways to live out one's gender—that male and female were not the only two realities.

I realize this may be a surprising thought if you have very little experience with gender variance. After all, many of us were raised in cultures that assume there are only two ways to live out our gender, as male or female. In fact, one of the first things we ask when we find out someone is pregnant is "Is it a boy or a girl?" We seldom stop to think that the baby might be intersex, two-spirit, or another gender identity. However, when discussing males and females getting married and divorcing, Jesus also mentions that there is another way, by birth or by choice, to live out one's gender—that gender variance, both biological and behavioral, is a reality.

In the next chapter we will give further consideration to the idea that, as Jesus implied, male and female are not the only two gender realities. For now, let us bring this chapter to a close by noting that the third significant thing about this passage from Matthew 19 is that, when Jesus mentions various ways that one ends up a eunuch, he does not condemn those ways or those people. Christ simply acknowledges eunuchs and the things that caused them to be that way as realities. This suggests that those of us who are Christ's followers today might want to do likewise—accept the realities of gender variance and not condemn gender variant individuals. (See Appendix A for suggestions of how to create a trans friendly congregation or group.)

part three

IMPLICIT VERSES AND ARGUMENTS

7

GENESIS 1:27 AND
THE ARGUMENT FROM CREATION

In an April 2015 interview with Diane Sawyer, former Olympic gold medalist and patriarch of the Kardashian clan Bruce Jenner revealed to the world that he had been dressing in women's clothes since he was nine years old and that he was now ready to live full time in his true gender identity. Shortly thereafter, I saw a Christian blog in which the topic of how the church should relate to transgender people was being discussed. Curious to see the responses, I logged on and began reading. While I saw numerous posts saying we should relate to trans individuals with the same love and acceptance Jesus offered to all people, the main argument I saw against God's (and therefore the church's) approval of trans folks was based on Genesis 1:27: "And God created man in his own image, in the image of God he created him; male and female he created them."

Based on this verse, some people concluded that God has created only two genders, so one is either male or female, and it would be a sin against God's created order to express oneself as anything other than strictly male or female. This means it would be sinful to express oneself in a gender queer manner, as androgynous, bigender, or two-spirit or as a cross-dresser. Others concluded that because God is the one who creates us, and God creates us anatomically either male or female, we don't get to "choose" which gender we are, because, again, that would be a sin against God's order of creation. This means it would be sinful for transgender people to change their external appearance through dress, mannerisms, or medical means to make it align more with their own internal sense of their gender identity. Let us consider each of these perspectives in turn.

When I was an elementary school librarian, I used to teach library and research skills to my students. I taught the younger students about the differences between the types of books we had in the library: about the picture books in the "everybody" section, the fiction books, our reference books, the biographies, and our nonfiction books. I would explain that the authors wrote these different types of books for different purposes, and that it was important that we keep that in mind when we were reading a book. When the students got older and started doing research I would ask them, "Which section should you choose your books from when you need to do research? Should you look in the fiction section?"

They would respond with a chorus of "No!"

"Should you look in the picture book section?"

Again they'd call out, "No!"

"So where should you look?" I'd ask. And of course, the correct response was in the nonfiction section, in biographies and in reference, because the authors had written those books for the purpose of giving their readers true facts and information (with the exception of the poetry section, 811 in the Dewey Decimal classification system, and the 398.2s, folk and fairy tales).

The Bible itself is actually a little library containing sixty-six books written by different authors during many different time periods. When reading the various books of the Bible, it is important for us to ask ourselves what I used to ask my young students, "What was the author's purpose in writing that book or that particular chapter?" Even a cursory reading of Genesis 1 reveals that this chapter is written as a poem, as a beautifully crafted literary reflection on the creation of the world. Each stanza begins with the immortal "And God said . . ." and ends with the beautiful "and there was morning and there was evening, the first day . . . the second day . . . the third day" and so on through all seven days.

Genesis 1 is such a poetic articulation of creation that I believe the author of Genesis was *not* trying to write a scientific explanation of the creation of all things. (Besides the poetic factor, there is also the fact that the scientific method had not yet been developed.) If I were explaining this to my young library students I would say it was not the author's intent to give us scientifically true facts and information in Genesis 1. Consequently, when interpreting the verses in this chapter, we must be very careful about arguing from silence, that is, we should be cautious about drawing a logical conclusion based on what the text does *not* state. This means that, just because Genesis 1 does not make a statement about a particular aspect of creation, this does not mean that reality does not exist in creation, nor that it is not part of God's *good* creation. For example, Genesis 1:3–5 says,

> And God said, "Let there be light," and there was light. God saw that the light was good, and he separated the light from the darkness. God called the light "day," and the darkness he called "night." And there was evening, and there was morning —the first day.

Taking this poetic passage literally and believing that it explained all the realities that God created regarding a twenty-four-hour period would result in us believing that there is nothing other than night or day. Of course, we know from experience that there is also dusk and dawn, those times of day when it is not totally day, but it is not totally night either.

Likewise, in Genesis 1:9–10 we find,

> And God said, "Let the water under the sky be gathered to one place, and let dry ground appear." And it was so. God

called the dry ground "land," and the gathered waters he called "seas." And God saw that it was good.

Again, taking this poetic passage literally and believing that it explained all the realities God created regarding land and sea would result in us believing that there is no such thing as shorelines or marshes, which can be under water during one part of a day and dry land hours later, depending on the tides. However, again we know from experience that this is not the case.

Another example of why we should view Genesis 1 as a poetic account of the creation of the world and not a factually accurate explanation has to do with the classification of living things. According to Genesis 1, all living things fit neatly into either the kingdom of plants, which God created on the third day (Gen. 1:11–13), or the kingdom of animals, which God created on the fifth and sixth days (Gen. 1:20–25). The biblical two-kingdom, plants and animals, classification system, for the most part, accurately describes the living organisms we see with our naked eyes on a daily basis.

However, scientists have realized that most microscopic organisms do not fit neatly into the limitations of a two-kingdom system. In 1866, Ernst Haeckel proposed adding a third kingdom of Protista. In 1938, Herbert Copeland argued that bacteria should be removed from Protista to create the fourth kingdom of Monera. In 1969, Robert Whittaker proposed that organisms be classified into five kingdoms: Monera (=bacteria), Protista (=mostly algae and protozoans), Plantae (=plants), Mycetae (=fungi) and Animalia (=animals). Whittaker's five kingdoms were the accepted scheme for the classification of organisms in science textbooks through the end of the twentieth century, but now American textbooks favor a six-kingdom classification system (replacing Monera with Bactera/Eubacteria and Archaea/Archaeabacteria), while the five-kingdom system is typically found in textbooks in Europe and other parts of the world.[1] For our purposes, it is important to note that even today, not all scientists agree on a five- or six-kingdom classification system, which suggests that, despite our best human efforts to categorize God's good creation, the reality is that the organisms God has created are infinitely more vast and varied than any of our finite human classification systems.

Which brings us to Genesis 1, verse 27. The poet writes,

> So God created man in his own image, in the image of God
> he created him; male and female he created them.

Some say this means God has created *only* male and female. But might there be a dawn and a dusk, a shoreline and a marshland, another classification kingdom in the realm of male and female? The reports of modern medicine answer this question with a resounding "Yes!"

INTERSEX PERSONS

Intersex persons are individuals born with external genitals and/or internal sexual reproductive organs and/or chromosomes that do not fit typical male or female patterns. According to MedlinePlus, the National Institutes of Health's (NIH's) website for lay people, intersex can be divided into four categories:

- 46, XX intersex. The person has the chromosomes of a woman, the ovaries of a woman, but external (outside) genitals that appear male. . . .

- 46, XY intersex. The person has the chromosomes of a man, but the external genitals are incompletely formed, ambiguous, or clearly female. Internally, testes may be normal, malformed, or absent. . . .

- True gonadal intersex. Here the person must have both ovarian and testicular tissue. This may be in the same gonad (an ovotestis), or the person might have one ovary and one testis. The person may have XX chromosomes, XY chromosomes, or both. The external genitals may be ambiguous or may appear to be female or male. . . .

- Complex or undetermined intersex disorders of sexual development. Many chromosome configurations other than simple 46, XX or 46, XY can result in disorders of sex development. . . . These disorders do not result in a condition where there is discrepancy between internal and external genitalia. However, there may be problems with sex hormone levels, overall sexual development, and altered numbers of sex chromosomes.[2]

In response to the question "How common are intersex conditions?" the American Psychological Association (APA) website states, "Some experts estimate that as many as 1 in every 1,500 babies is born with genitals that cannot easily be classified as male or female."[3] A more detailed response to this question can be found at the Intersex Society of North America (ISNA) website: "If you ask experts at medical centers how often a child is born so noticeably atypical in terms of genitalia that a specialist in sex differentiation is called in, the number comes out to about 1 in 1500 to 1 in 2000 births. But a lot more people than that are born with subtler forms of sex anatomy variations, some of which won't show up until later in life."[4]

"Later in life" is often at puberty. Consider the case of someone born with 46, XY intersex. As stated in the preceding description, "the person has the chromosomes of a man, but the external genitals are incompletely formed, ambiguous, or clearly female. Internally, testes may be normal, malformed, or absent. . . ." This means that some persons are born with clearly female genitals, so are assigned "female" at birth and raised as girls. But internally, they have male chromosomes and perhaps normal testes, but not ovaries or a uterus. Consequently, when they reach puberty, these individuals who are being raised as girls, based on their external genitals, never get their periods. This is the point, "later in life," when further medical examinations reveal that this person is intersex. Consequently, it is important to realize that many intersex conditions do not manifest themselves at birth.

Reading further on the ISNA website reveals that an extensive review of the medical literature from 1955 to 1998 was published in 2000. The researchers who conducted this review gathered information on how frequently the various manifestations of intersex, not only those that were visible at birth, occurred. After compiling all their data these researchers concluded that the "total number of people whose bodies differ from standard male or female [is] one in 100 births."[5] Let me repeat that.

Total number of people whose bodies differ from standard male or female [is] one in 100 births.

This means there are many, *many* individuals whom God has created intersex, individuals who have one of the various realities in the preceding list that make them neither strictly male nor typically female but a slightly different gender in God's good creation. Sadly, many intersex persons report that either they and/or their parents were told by their doctors "not to talk about this," which is why most of us are not aware of the intersex reality today. Likewise, many were also told by their doctors, "You're the only person I know of like this," which led to feelings of freakishness and extreme isolation.[6] Fortunately, thanks to the Internet, there are now online as well as face-to-face support groups for intersex persons and their families, which is allowing them to connect and to work together for social, political, and medical reforms.[7]

This evidence shows that intersex conditions are the dusk and dawn of God's male and female creations. They are the shoreline and the marshland of gender. Like the differences in kingdom classifications, they are hard to see with the naked eye, but they are real, and they do exist. People whose physiology is different from typical male/female physiology are part of God's creation . . . part of God's *good* creation.

Therefore, we can no longer argue that being any of the gender variant expressions under the transgender umbrella is "a sin" based on the notion that God creates only male and female, because we now know that God creates at least four different categories of intersex conditions, resulting in approximately one in every one hundred persons being born intersex.

"THE FALL" PERSPECTIVE

Personally, I take the perspective that intersex conditions are part of God's good creation and further evidence of the incredible creativity and unfathomable imagination of an infinite God. However, there are other Christians who see the physical realities of intersex conditions and the cognitive/psychological realities of the transgender experience as evidence of "the Fall."[8] This line of thinking suggests that, while God originally made all things good, as a result of Adam and Eve's sin in the Garden of Eden (commonly referred to as "the Fall"; see Genesis 3), everything is now broken, so bodies and brains no longer always function in the good way God intended. Consequently, we end up with babies being born with cleft palates, club feet, Down syndrome, or intersex conditions, and with people suffering from chemical depression, schizophrenia, or gender identities that do not match the gender they were assigned at birth.

If we were to follow this line of thinking one step further, the next logical question we would ask is, "How should we respond to these fallen conditions, to these medical conditions that are less than the good that God intended in creation?" In the cases just mentioned, most Christians (except for those who do not believe in any medical intervention at all) would say that we should use all the medical wisdom God has given us to help restore these individuals to mental and physical health and wholeness. This is considered the normal, humane course of treatment for every one of these conditions—*except* in the case of transgender individuals. When it comes to gender variant individuals, many people frown upon therapeutic support and the hormonal and surgical treatments that bring greater mental and physical health and wholeness to trans people. Why is this?

I believe the answer to this question is because, culturally, we have yet to accept that gender variance is a "normal" part of the human experience. For the most part, society still sees someone who is gender variant as a person who is "abnormal" and who needs to be "fixed." However, therapists have spent years trying to "fix" transgender individuals, only to have the American Psychological Association conclude:

> A psychological state is considered a mental disorder only if it causes significant distress or disability. Many transgender people do not experience their gender as distressing or disabling, which implies that identifying as transgender does not constitute a mental disorder. For these individuals, the significant problem is finding affordable resources, such as counseling, hormone therapy, medical procedures, and the social support necessary to freely express their gender identity and minimize discrimination. Many other obstacles may lead to distress, including a lack of acceptance within society, direct or indirect experiences with discrimination, or assault. These experiences may lead many transgender people to suffer with anxiety, depression, or related disorders at higher rates than nontransgender persons.[9]

In other words, through their extensive experiences with transgender people, psychologists have realized that the problem with transgender people is *not being transgender.* The problem is *not being accepted and supported and allowed access to the things that all of us need as human beings*: housing, medical treatment, opportunities to earn an income, loving relationships, supportive spiritual communities, and safe environments in which to work and play. Consequently, I believe that Christians who view intersex conditions and the transgender experience as a result of the Fall should also take very seriously their responsibility to offer redemption to gender variant individuals—acts of redemption that, based on the APA's findings, might look like advocating for the full civil rights of these people and full inclusion in all aspects of the body of Christ.

GENDER IDENTITY AND "CHOICE"

Having briefly considered things from "the Fall" perspective, now let us look at more possibilities related to the perspective that God's good creation is incredibly diverse and that it includes gender variant individuals. Christians who are not comfortable with this inclusive perspective might concede that if God created a person to be intersex, then it would be okay for that person to "choose" their gender identity. However, they would maintain that it would be a sin for persons whom God does create with typically male or female physiology to choose their gender identity; it would be a sin against God's natural order of creation.[10] This line of argument has several inherent assumptions, so in order for this argument to be valid, we must agree to its assumptions. These assumptions are:

1. Our bodies are somehow more indicative of who we are than our personalities, our minds, spirits, souls . . . whatever word(s) you want to use to describe that internal essence that makes each person a unique individual.

2. God creates our bodies, but not our minds/souls/personalities/spirits/essence.

3. It is a sin to make changes to the body God has created.

4. It is a sin to make changes to the gender God has created.

Let us consider the first of these assumptions.

American cultural practice suggests that we believe that our internal essence is actually more indicative of who we are than is our bodies. For example, spouses do not divorce their partners just because they lose a leg to diabetes or a limb serving in the military. Part of the reason they do not do this is because they believe that who their spouse is on the inside is more important than their outside. Likewise, when our friends change their bodies by choosing to lose large amounts of weight, or have cosmetic surgery or a Botox injection, we don't think they are a different person, someone we need to get to know all over again. No, we believe that who they are on the inside is more constant than who they are on the outside. As a society, we often act on the assumptions that a person's internal essence is more important than and more constant than their external selves. In other words, we assume that our essence, not our body, is indicative of who we are.

Granted, as a culture, we are not consistent with this belief. The fact that euthanasia is not legal indicates that, when it comes to the matter of life and death, we give priority to the body over the essence. However, the fact that our culture allows for "do not resuscitate" (DNR) orders indicates that we believe persons "of sound mind" should have jurisdiction over their bodies in matters of life and death, another indicator that, even here, we lean towards a person's essence being more indicative than their body of who they are. So, given that Americans believe our internal essence is more indicative of who we are than is our external anatomy, why are we reluctant to apply this same belief to matters of gender?

Which brings us to our second consideration: Does God create our bodies, but not our minds/souls/personalities/spirits/essences? While Christians disagree about many things, I have never heard of any who would say that God creates our bodies, but not our souls, our essences. Similarly, parents of more than one child will tell you that babies enter this world with an essence, with a personality, and that each of their children are unique . . . and have been from the very beginning! Those of the Catholic faith urge infant baptism, especially if there is a possibility that the baby might die, so the baby's soul will be saved. Regardless of one's view on this Catholic doctrine, I raise the point here to indicate the common assumption that babies are born with souls, with something that make them unique, particular, special—something innate and internal—some essence created by God.

Now let us consider our third assumption: It is a sin to make changes to the body God has created. Obviously, we do not believe this, since we make changes to our bodies all the time—for the sake of our physical health, and/or for the sake of our mental health and well-being. For example, many people get tummy tucks, facelifts, breast implants or hair transplants to improve their mental health and align their external image of themselves with their internal image. Hair dressers straighten, perm, or dye hair daily, and no one objects, nor does anyone complain about dental practices that engage in teeth whitening or orthodontics. Likewise, we spend billions of dollars each year on over-the-counter and prescription drugs to help us feel better physically and/or mentally and, again, no one objects to us using such drugs and chemicals to alter our bodies.

However, when transgender individuals want to use prescription drugs (hormone replacement therapy—HRT) to alter their bodies, some people object. And while it is okay for a cisgender (a person whose gender identity *does* match the gender they were assigned at birth) woman to have breast implants to align her internal image of herself with her external presentation, many people say it is wrong for a trans woman to do exactly the same thing. Likewise, many would say it is not a sin to reshape the nose God gave us, but it *is* a sin to reshape the genitals God gave us. Personally, I think it is very important that we carefully consider, since we have no objections to people altering their bodies surgically or chemically for the sake of physical or mental health, why it is that so many object when the reason people want to alter their bodies has to do with gender?

At this point, some might say, "Well obviously, improving one's physical and mental health are good and legitimate reasons for altering one's body with surgery or drugs; God wants us to be healthy, happy, and whole. However, messing with our bodies because our gender identity does not match our genitals is not a legitimate reason." However, the fact that, according to a 2011 survey, a staggering 41 percent of gender variant individuals have attempted suicide[11] indicates that aligning one's outward appearance with one's inward sense of one's gender identity is definitely a matter of mental and physical health, and even a matter of life and death!

Which brings us to our fourth assumption, the one that appears to finally be the real crux of the problem, the assumption that it is a sin to mess with the gender God gave us. But how do we *know* what gender God gave us? Is our gender determined by our *external* genitals or by our *internal* gender identity—our innate sense of whether our true essence is more male, more female, a combination of both, or neither? If we say that our genitals determine our gender, then what does that mean for those intersex individuals whose genitals are not typically male or female? How is their gender to be determined? And if, as we previously discussed, our internal sense of ourselves is considered to be more indicative of who we are than are our bodies (as in the case of amputees and those who have had cosmetic surgery), then this may be the case when it comes to gender also. In other words, perhaps the divinely created determinant of our gender is not our external genitals but our internal gender identity!

Such a perspective answers the question of how to determine the gender of an intersex person—let them determine it for themselves, based on their innate sense of their own gender. The possibility that gender is determined internally and not externally is also consistent with the growing number of testimonies of the parents of trans children. These parents are reporting that as early as the innocent ages of two, three, four, and five their children have been telling them that they are not the gender they are being raised as—based on their genitals—but that they are the opposite gender! Such pronouncements have absolutely confounded their parents who have been faithfully raising, dressing, and treating their children as the gender suggested by that child's genitals!

TRANSGENDER CHILDREN

Jazz Jennings is the most documented trans child in the world. Jazz was born in 2000. In 2007 she was one of three transgender children and their families interviewed by Barbara Walters on *20/20*. That same year, her parents were interviewed for an *ABC News* article by Alan B. Goldberg and Joneil Adriano. The journalists wrote:

> From the moment he could speak, Jazz made it clear he wanted to wear a dress. At only 15 months, he would unsnap his onesies to make it look like a dress. When his parents praised Jazz as a "good boy," he would correct them, saying he was a good girl.
>
> The Jennings wanted to believe it would pass. Scott [Jazz's father] said he "was in a bit of denial" about what Jazz was trying to tell them. After all, even their rowdy twin boys, who are two years older than Jazz, had painted their nails growing up. But Jazz kept gravitating to girl things, insisting that his penis was a mistake.
>
> When Jazz was two, he asked his mother a question that left her numb and frozen. "[He] said, 'Mommy, when's the good fairy going to come with her magic wand and change, you know, my genitalia?'" according to Renee.[12]

After a therapist who specialized in sex and gender issues confirmed that Jazz had all the signs of being transgender,

> the Jennings explained the situation to their other children. In their home, they came to accept Jazz as a girl. There he could wear a dress or dance as a ballerina, although they still referred to Jazz with male pronouns.
>
> In public, they kept Jazz's look more ambiguous or gender neutral, especially at preschool, where he was allowed to put on a pretty top but he had to wear pants. Officially, Jazz remained a boy.
>
> Jazz chafed under that arrangement. He wasn't happy until he could present as a girl both indoors and outdoors. Everyday became a struggle, according to Renee. Finally, a dance recital opened the Jennings' eyes to just how unhappy Jazz was.

"She wasn't allowed to wear a tutu, like the rest of the girls. And she just kind of stood there and snapped her finger and did the tapping thing with the toe, and just looked so sad," Renee recalled. "It was heartbreaking to watch. Really heartbreaking."

The dance recital was a turning point. The Jennings then made the difficult decision to let their son become their daughter. On his fifth birthday, Jazz wore a girl's one-piece bathing suit. "He" was now "she," and an innocent pool party became a "coming out" to all of her friends.[13]

Now, as a teenager, Jazz has become an active advocate, role model and spokesperson for the transgender community. In 2016, she starred in *I Am Jazz,* a reality TV show about her life.

Marlo Mack (pen name), mother of M, another young trans girl, recently wrote an op-ed piece for *The Advocate.* In it (and in her wonderful *GenderMom* blog), she describes some of her family's experience:

My child, at age 3, told me she was a girl. She looked me in the eyes and said, "Mama, something went wrong in your tummy that made me come out as a boy instead of a girl."

Since age 2, she'd been begging me to dress her in the pretty clothes she saw little girls wearing and had been obsessed with the things little girls often love, like princesses and fairies and the color pink. At first I assumed the whole thing was a phase. I said she could like pink and play with dolls, but that she had a boy body, so she was a boy. When she kept asserting her girlhood, I did what parents do—I went looking for advice from the experts. . . .

In every case, the experts I consulted had the same response to my questions. They didn't know. They . . . admitted that there wasn't really any reliable research on kids like mine.

So I had to wing it. . . .

Early on . . . I tried to encourage more "masculine" activities, suggesting karate classes when she wanted to sign up for ballet (we compromised on co-ed gymnastics). . . . I encouraged more play dates with boys and more time with her dad.

But ultimately, I couldn't stomach the idea of denying my child the things she loved nor bear to see her so unhappy. . . .

My real turning point came about a year after she first told me she was a girl. I attended a support group for the parents of transgender and gender-nonconforming kids and heard a story that kept me up at night for weeks afterward. A young mother sat across the table from me, sobbing her heart out as she told us what had happened to her 5-year-old when a local psychologist advised a regimen. . . .

"I took away all his dolls, all his most favorite things. I told him he was a boy and that's that, because that's what the doctor said to do," she said. Within a couple of months, her kindergartener had stopped speaking and was diagnosed with severe depression. "I almost lost him," she said.

The story haunted me because my child had recently begun a similar disappearing act. After months of fighting me ("I'm a girl!"), the kid was giving up. She stopped correcting me when I used her hated "boy name," shrugged when I suggested karate lessons yet again. . . . Another mom in the support group witnessed the same phenomenon in her child and described it perfectly: "My 4-year-old looked like a tired old man."

I decided that enough was enough. I sat my child down, looked her in the eyes, and asked the question one last time: "Do you really want to be a girl?"

"I don't want to be a girl, Mama," she said. "I am a girl."

Three years on, I am the mother of a stunningly happy and confident 7-year-old transgender daughter. She is excelling academically, popular at school, and generally thriving on all fronts.[14]

I share Jazz's and M's stories at length to demonstrate that the parents who are allowing their children to transition at young ages are not irresponsible, laissez-faire, misguided, deluded individuals. They are loving, caring, intelligent, protective, and proactive parents. They are moms and dads who have armed themselves with as much information as they can find, sought and taken professional advice, have tried valiantly to redirect their children to gender conforming behavior and interests, and have lost as much sleep as any of us would if our three-year-old was telling us, "No Mommy. No Daddy. I'm not a boy, I'm a girl!"

A Google search on the Internet reveals that there are multitudes of trans children just like M and Jazz, children who by the innocent ages of three, four, and five were telling their astounded parents that they were not the gender indicated by their genitals. Granted, there are also very young children who go through phases of cross-sex behavior. How do we know that children like M and Jazz are really transgender? Dr. Johanna Olson is a pediatrician and medical director at the Center for Transyouth Health and Development at Children's Hospital Los Angeles, the largest transgender youth clinic in the United States.[15] The mom of a transgender daughter reports that at the 2015 Gender Odyssey conference Dr. Joanna responded to the question, "How can you tell which kids are transgender and which are just gender non-conforming?" in this way:

> Dr. Jo: "Unfortunately, there's no blood test for transgender."
>
> But she explains that there are clues. She refers to these clues as "Predictors of Persistence." The kids who are likely to "persist" in identifying as transgender often (though not always) look like this:
>
> Dr. Jo: "They say they ARE another gender, as opposed to saying 'I wish I were another gender.'"
>
> Dr. Jo: "They're really distressed by their gender. These are kids who are trying to cut their body parts off with nail clippers, dental floss, scissors. These are kids who take baths with leg-

gings on. There's a lot of self-harm and suicidality, because walking around and not being authentic feels really, really bad for them."

Dr. Jo: "Underwear and bathing suits are a big difference between kids who just want to dress like another gender and kids who tell us they really ARE another gender. It's really common for transgender kids to ask for underwear that matches the gender they identify with."

Dr. Jo: "When you ask them how they see themselves in the future, as a grown-up, it's not the gender they were assigned at birth."

Dr. Jo: "In pretend fantasy play, like when they're playing house, or creating an avatar for a computer game, these kids will take on the gender they identify with."

Dr. Jo emphasized that these are just clues, and that there are no hard-and-fast rules for identifying a transgender child. The best thing we can do, she said, is simply to listen to them. "Nobody knows your own gender better than you do, and that goes for children, too."[16]

Likewise, transgender individuals who have transitioned as adults also testify that they knew, at these same early ages, that something about their gender was different. Now, when adults come out as transgender, I understand how people might be inclined to think that something so different, something so out of the norm, must be the result of some dysfunction somewhere along the line. But two- and three-year-olds are so innocent that, personally, I believe they are speaking not out of dysfunction but out of their purity and innocence. I believe they are speaking their truth. And my belief that they are speaking their truth inclines me to believe that transgender adults who say they have always known, since they too were innocent children, are also speaking out of the truth of their divinely created being, and not out of any dysfunction.

WHAT DETERMINES GENDER?

So let's return to our discussion. Exactly what is it that determines gender? The testimony of these trans children and the testimony of transgender adults indicates that for them, it certainly is not genitals. Nor can it be genitals for intersex persons, because their reproductive anatomy is often neither typically male nor strictly female. Consequently, it appears that, for at least some people, genitals do *not* determine gender. To put that another way, for at least some people, their divinely created genitals do *not* determine their divinely created gender.

In response to the question about what determines gender, even the medical community does not currently have a definitive answer. Dr. Jo notes that

> We don't know what causes someone to be transgender, but what we're learning as we're putting the pieces together is that there are likely many factors. Genetics, hormones or other elements likely play a role. The information that is being discovered now is indicating that the neural wiring in a transgender person's brain looks more similar to their gender of identity rather than their gender of assignment at birth. What this means is that gender identity is most likely developing in the womb. Much more needs to be explored in order to understand gender identity information.[17]

I realize that what you have just read here about intersex people and transgender two-year-olds and gender-related neural wiring may be very new information to many of you. Like myself and many others, you may have just always assumed that genitals determine gender because that has been our experience for most of our lives. And let's face it, our belief in a two-gender system—male and female—is about as core a belief as most of us have. In fact, our culture even has a name for this belief. We call it the "gender binary." Dictionary.com, defines "gender binary" as

1. a classification system consisting of two genders, male and female.

2. a concept or belief that there are only two genders, male and female.

I think it is important for us to note that the dictionary does not define "gender binary" as "a scientifically proven fact" or "a divinely ordered reality" but as a "classification system" and "a concept or belief." I shared previously about the way our binary "plant or animal" classification system has shifted to a five- or six-entity classification system because of information scientists now know that could not be seen earlier with just the naked eye. So we know that classification systems change based on new information.

GOD CALLS PEOPLE TO SHIFT THEIR BELIEFS

Likewise, we have many biblical examples of God calling people to shift their beliefs and open their minds to new concepts. We've already discussed how, throughout the history of the Bible, God called God's people to change their views on eunuchs. God called Abraham and Sarah to change their perspective and believe they could have a child in their old age (Gen. 18:1–15). God called the Israelites to change their perspective and believe they could go in and possess the Promised Land (Num. 13–14). God called the people of Jesus' day to change their views and believe that it is not what goes into a person's mouth, but what comes out of someone's mouth that makes a person unclean (Matt. 15:10–20). God continued to call the people of Jesus' day to change their understanding of sin and punishment through Jesus' pardoning of the woman caught in adultery (John 8:1–11) and Jesus' healing of the man born blind (John 9).

Remember that story? Jesus and his disciples entered a town where they met a man who had been blind since birth. Jesus' disciples immediately asked Jesus a question based on the common beliefs of the day, "Who sinned, this man or his parents, that he was born blind?"

(Today people ask similar questions about transgender children and their parents: "What's wrong with that child?" or "What did the parents of that child do wrong?") In response to his disciples' questions, Jesus called people to change their beliefs when he answered, "Neither this man nor his parents sinned, but this happened so that the works of God might be displayed in him." (See chapter 10 for further thoughts on this verse.)

God also called Peter to make a radical change in his beliefs about what was clean and unclean, what was sinful and what was not, a shift in perspective that changed the course of history. Because of Peter's dream, where he heard God telling him to "kill and eat" the unclean animals, and his subsequent experience of seeing God pour out the Holy Spirit on Cornelius and his family, "the Way" that Jesus taught morphed from a small Jewish movement into a world religion for Gentiles as well (Acts 10–11:18).

Likewise, God called Saul to change his perspective on Jesus, a shift in beliefs that changed Saul, the devout Pharisee and persecutor of Christians, into the world-changing Paul, apostle to the Gentiles (Acts 9). The testimony of scripture is that God is continually calling people to change their beliefs. Could it be that God is now calling us to change our perspective about the gender binary and believe that God creates more than just male and female and that *all* God's creations are *good*?

Many people have already made this change. As of this writing, there are now eleven different countries—Ireland, Malta, Australia, Bangladesh, New Zealand, Germany, India, Nepal, Columbia, Argentina, and Denmark —that offer some sort of third gender option on their citizens' passports. Out of respect for their intersex and transgender citizens, each of these countries has shifted its perspective on the gender binary.[18]

If the reading of this book is your first exposure to information about the TQI in the LGBTQI acronym, if this is your first time learning information about people who are transgender, gender queer, or intersex, then you may be experiencing a variety of responses. You may be laughing in disbelief, like Sarah, when God's messengers said she'd have a baby in her old age, or shaking your head in confusion, like Peter, when God said to him in his dream to kill and eat all the nonkosher animals. You might be thinking, "No gender binary? No only male and female? That's just crazy! That's ridiculous!" Such thoughts are not surprising, as many new ideas sound far-fetched when we first entertain them. However, just because this is our normal human reaction to new ideas, it does not mean that such ideas are therefore wrong. It simply means that they are new. To offer the clichéd example, the people of Columbus' day thought his idea about a round world was crazy . . . but that does not mean it was wrong. In your attempt to contemplate the idea of a gender nonbinary world you might even be thinking, "What would that do to our society? Surely this would be the end of civilization as we know it!" Just remember, eleven countries, eleven societies have already made this shift in their thinking and established it in their passport laws, and the societal results have been so unharmful, the consequences have been so *not* dire, that most of us didn't even know about it!

· · ·

In the beginning, God created. Throughout the course of this chapter, we have seen that the infinite God has created a world so infinite in its diversity that it cannot be adequately described by the binary plant or animal system suggested by the poetry of Genesis 1. Likewise, we have seen that the male or female gender binary classification system suggested by Genesis 1:27 is inadequate to describe the reality of the approximately one out of every one hundred persons born with one of the varieties of intersex conditions. It is also inadequate to describe the reality of those born with the innate knowledge that their internal gender identity does not match their external genitals. While it is never easy to change perceptions and adopt new beliefs, the evidence that God creates genders beyond strictly male or female is as compelling as the beauty of our marshlands and shorelines; it is as real as the dusk and dawn of each new day.

8

MATTHEW 16:13-27 AND THE NOTION OF "CHOICE"

When it comes to being gender variant, there *is* a choice involved. Johanna Olson, MD, medical director of the Center for Transyouth Health and Development at Children's Hospital Los Angeles, describes it this way in an online video entitled "When parents don't support their transgender child":

> They [parents] really need to understand that you're born with your gender identity. It's an immutable characteristic and part of your core being and that your gender identity is not a choice. The choice piece of it is the choice you make about how to live authentically. The choice that you make is what you're going to express to the world around you. They're not making a choice about their internal gender.[1]

What Dr. Johanna said about choosing to live authentically reminded me of a sermon I had preached several years earlier. I include it here, as preached, as evidence that the Bible supports all people choosing to live an authentic life, a life that is consistent with who God created and calls us to be. I also include it as an example to ministers and chaplains of how we can incorporate examples from and of transgender lives in our preaching in order to make our congregations or chapel services more trans friendly. (See Appendix A for more suggestions.) I opened that sermon with the same joke I shared in chapter 2, so, please, just enjoy it again!

· · ·

SERMON: "DENY *WHICH* SELF?"

MATTHEW 16:13-27
preached at City of Light Atlanta, July 14, 2013

> [13]When Jesus came to the region of Caesarea Philippi, he asked his disciples, "Who do people say the Son of Man is?"
>
> [14]They replied, "Some say John the Baptist; others say Elijah; and still others, Jeremiah or one of the prophets."
>
> [15]"But what about you?" he asked. "Who do you say I am?"
>
> [16]Simon Peter answered, "You are the Messiah, the Son of the living God."
>
> [17]Jesus replied, "Blessed are you, Simon son of Jonah, for this was not revealed to you by flesh and blood, but by my Father in heaven. [18]And I tell you that you are Peter, and on this rock I will build my church, and the gates of Hades will not overcome it. [19]I will give you the keys of the kingdom of heaven; whatever you bind on earth will be bound in heaven, and whatever you loose on earth will be loosed in heaven." [20]Then he ordered his disciples not to tell anyone that he was the Messiah.
>
> [21]From that time on Jesus began to explain to his disciples that he must go to Jerusalem and suffer many things at the hands of the elders, the chief priests and the teachers of the law, and that he must be killed and on the third day be raised to life.
>
> [22]Peter took him aside and began to rebuke him. "Never, Lord!" he said. "This shall never happen to you!"
>
> [23]Jesus turned and said to Peter, "Get behind me, Satan! You are a stumbling block to me; you do not have in mind the concerns of God, but merely human concerns."
>
> [24]Then Jesus said to his disciples, "Whoever wants to be my disciple must deny themselves and take up their cross and follow me. [25]For whoever wants

to save their life will lose it, but whoever loses their life for me will find it. [26]What good will it be for someone to gain the whole world, yet forfeit their soul? Or what can anyone give in exchange for their soul? [27]For the Son of Man is going to come in his Father's glory with his angels, and then he will reward each person according to what they have done.

Once upon a time a there was a person who needed guidance from God, so they decided to open up the Bible and listen for God's word.

They closed their eyes, opened the pages, stuck their finger down and read, "Judas went out and hung himself."

Not being entirely certain what to make of that, they decided to try again. So for a second time they opened the Bible, stuck their finger down, and this time they read, "Go thou and do likewise!"

This story is a humorous illustration of one of the truths my seminary professors taught me: C-I-E—context is *everything*! This means that if we try to apply one single scripture verse to our lives without looking at it in the context of the whole passage in which it appears, we're liable to end up with an interpretation of that verse that is far, far removed from what God originally intended.

I believe that is what has happened to many of us regarding our Gospel text for this morning: "Deny yourself, take up your cross and follow me." Taken out of its context, it's easy to interpret this verse to mean that who we are is somehow inherently bad or wrong, and that in order to please God we should never do what makes us happy; we should never pursue the deepest desires of our hearts. Instead, we should sacrifice ourselves for others, put the needs of everyone else first, and take no thought or responsibility for our own self-care. But *is* that what Jesus is saying here, or does the context of this verse possibly reveal just the opposite message? Let's take a look and see.

According to the Gospel writer, right before Jesus told his followers to "Deny themselves, take up their cross and follow me," Jesus had been trying to find out from the disciples if they had yet come to the place of understanding that he was indeed, the Christ—which is the Greek word for the Hebrew word "Messiah"—the Christ, the Messiah, the promised one who, according to Jewish tradition, was to come and reestablish the glorious kingdom of Israel. So after asking them who others were saying he was, Jesus says, "But what about *you*? Who do *you* say that I am?"

And that's when Peter gives his famous response.

¹⁶Simon Peter answered, "You are the Christ, the Messiah, the Son of the living God."

¹⁷Jesus replied, "Blessed are you, Simon son of Jonah, for this was not revealed to you by flesh and blood, but by my Father in heaven. And I tell you that you are Peter, and on this rock I will build my church."

Jesus is delighted with Peter's response, thrilled that he's finally gotten it! So Jesus says, "Blessed are you, Simon son of Jonah, for this was not revealed to you by flesh and blood but by my Father in heaven."

Then Jesus says, "And I tell you that you are Peter, and on this rock I will build my church." What Jesus is doing here—when he says, "I tell you that you are Peter, and on this rock I will build my church"—what's happening here is that Jesus is having some fun with Peter's name. Jesus is engaging in a little word play with the name "Peter" and the statement that Peter has just made. You see, in Greek, the word for "Peter" is *petros*, which means "rock." So what Jesus is suggesting here with his word play is that the words Peter has just said are representative of Peter's true identity. Jesus says, "You are Peter. Your true self is solid, rocklike." And this truth that Peter has just proclaimed, that Jesus is the Messiah, this truth is also the rock, the solid foundation upon which the whole church will be built.

Jesus is delighted that his followers have finally understood that he is the Messiah. And now that the disciples have finally gotten *that*, Jesus begins to stretch their understanding of who the Messiah is to be. You see, in those days, the Jewish people expected their Messiah to be a great military leader—one who would be mighty in battle and vanquish their foes—and at that time, their foes were the Romans who occupied their land. Everyone in Jesus' day expected the Messiah to overthrow the Romans and reestablish the kingdom of Israel to its former glory. But Jesus knew that was not God's plan for who the Messiah would be; Jesus knew he was the Christ, the Messiah, but that his life would play out very differently. So . . . according to the gospel writer,

²¹From that time on Jesus began to explain to his disciples that he must go to Jerusalem and suffer many things and that he must be killed, and on the third day be raised to life.

Well, this did not fit with the disciples' understanding of who the Messiah was to be *at all*. "A dead Messiah? A Christ who gets killed? No, that's not how this story goes! That's not what we've learned from the teachings of our religious leaders. The Messiah doesn't die. The Christ kills our enemies and then we all live happily ever after!"

This was the common understanding of the people of Jesus' day, and it was that human understanding that Peter was operating under when he takes Jesus aside and says to him, "This shall never happen to you!" Now notice the name Jesus uses for Peter when he responds to him here. Notice how Peter goes from being a solid rock, who speaks truth, to being a stumbling block who gets in the way!

> 23Jesus turned and said to Peter, "Get behind me, Satan! You are a stumbling block to me; you do not have in mind the concerns of God, but merely human concerns."
>
> Then Jesus said to his disciples, "Whoever wants to be my disciple must deny themselves and take up their cross and follow me.

And that's when Jesus turns and says to the disciples, "If you would come after me, you must deny your self, take up your cross and follow me." Understood in its context, the self that Jesus is asking his followers to deny here is the self that Peter is currently expressing, not the *true* self, the solid, *petros* self whom Jesus praised for speaking the truth just a few short verses ago. No! The self that Jesus tells his disciples to deny here is the self that causes Jesus to actually refer to Peter as Satan! It's the self that looks at things from a human perspective, in contrast to the self that looks at things from God's perspective.

In this case, it's Peter's false self that he is to deny, the self that clings to old traditional religious teachings instead of being open to the new thing that God is doing. The self that Peter is to deny is the misguided self that holds on to the human notion that military might is what will create a great nation instead of embracing Jesus' teachings about loving one's enemies.

Jesus further clarifies this idea that the self we are to deny is the self that looks at things from a human perspective instead of from God's perspective when he adds to the directive "deny yourself" the words "and take up your cross and follow me." You see, in Jesus' day, a cross represented worldly thought, the human reward system. If you did not play by the rules of the Jewish religious authorities or if you did not conform to the values of the Roman Empire, then you ended up on a cross. So this injunction to "take up your cross" does not mean to choose to suffer the pain of denying your true self. Nor does it mean that we are to deny our own needs and suffer the pain of doing and doing and overdoing for others.

What Jesus means here is that we are to be willing to suffer the pain that comes from not playing by all of society's rules, the pain we'll experience as a result of rejecting misguided human value systems in order to follow Christ's teachings. What Jesus is referring to is the kind of pain Martin Luther King experienced when he challenged the value systems of America in the 1950s and '60s, the kind of pain transgender people suffer when they come out in our society today. Here Jesus is telling his followers that this is what we're signing up for when we deny our misguided, false selves and challenge the world's values by taking up our crosses and following him.

Then, in the next couple of verses, Jesus expands on this notion of our two different selves by saying,

> [25]For whoever wants to save their life will lose it, but whoever loses their life for me will find it. [26]What good will it be for a person if they gain the whole world yet forfeit their soul? And what can a person give in exchange for their soul?"

When I ponder these words in this context I hear Jesus saying that we have a soul self, a true self, a God-created, God-aligned self that God desires for us to honor, to save. We may be tempted to think that we need to live our lives by the world's rules, to do the things others want us to do in order to conform to the reward system of our culture, but Jesus is saying here that if we do that, we will lose at life, not win; we will forfeit our soul self and be unfaithful to God by dishonoring the unique self that God created us to be. "What will it profit a person if they gain the whole world"—if we get all the goodies the world promises us if we play by its rules—"yet lose their soul,"—sacrifice our true selves in order to do that? Two selves . . . a soul self and a worldly self; a self that looks at things from God's perspective and a self that looks at things from a human perspective. The self that Jesus calls people to deny here is not our soul self, our true identity, but that part of our self that still tries to evaluate things using the value system of this world.

That means that Jesus is not saying what we twenty-first-century Christians commonly interpret this passage to mean when we take it out of context. Jesus isn't saying, "Only do for others. Don't think about your own needs." Jesus is *not* saying, "Go out and hang yourself" which is pretty much what happens when we just give and give and give, and don't exercise good self-care. We end up killing ourselves, our true selves. And that's exactly the *opposite* of what Jesus is telling us to do here!

Instead, what Jesus is saying here, in this context—where he follows the statement "Deny yourself, take up your cross and follow me" with the question "What does it profit a person if they gain the whole world but lose their soul?"—in this context, what Jesus is saying is "Deny the value system of this world in order to live according to my ways, which is according to your true identity, your soul self."

Friends, did you hear this good news? This is *not* a passage about how we are to relate to others. This is Jesus' teaching about how we are to relate to our selves—to our false self, the self that has been indoctrinated with the values of this world, and our true self, our soul self—the self that is the made in the image of God, the self that is the one unique, beautiful facet of the amazing Divine Diamond!

And then Jesus takes this teaching about how we are to relate to ourselves one step further. In our scripture reading for this morning—did you notice how it ended? Right after Jesus asks, "What good will it be for someone to gain the whole world, yet forfeit their soul? Or what can anyone give in exchange for their soul?" Jesus says,

> 27For the Son of Man is going to come in his Father's glory with his angels,
> and then he will reward each person according to what they have done."

So here, in the context of this passage, Jesus says that not only are we to live according to our true selves, but that our reward will actually be based on how well we do that.

Did you hear that? This is serious stuff!

This is Jesus' invitation to each of us to look deep down in our souls and be honest with ourselves about who we really are. To be honest about our sexual orientation, our gender identity, our unique gifts, our particular and peculiar vocational desires. And, folks, I probably don't have to tell you that what we find when we go looking for our true selves doesn't always fit with the value system of this world; it doesn't always make those around us happy!

When Jesus started living out his truth—that he was to be a Messiah who established a realm of radically inclusive love—it made the keepers of the religious value system of his day so unhappy that they hung him on a cross.

When Rosa Parks started living out her truth—that she had as much right to sit in the front of the bus as anyone else—it challenged the cultural values of her day and ignited a civil rights movement.

In the movie *Chariots of Fire*, when gold medalist Eric Liddell claimed his truth, that when he ran he felt the glory of God, it made his sister unhappy because she thought he should be serving on the mission field and not training for the Olympics.

When my college roommate claimed her truth, that she had the gifts and graces and deep desire to be a teacher, it made her parents very unhappy because they wanted her to be a doctor.

When my daughter's college roommate claimed her truth, that she's homosexual, her parents kicked her out of their house because they want her to be heterosexual.

When my transgender friend claimed her truth, that her internal gender identity did not match her external appearance, her spouse told her she was being selfish.

And that spouse is right. My friend *is* being "self-ish"—and thank God she is! Thank God that she and all these other people I just mentioned had the faith to look into their souls and see the true selves God has created and called them to be, and then had the courage to live self-ishly, to live out of their truth even though it made others unhappy because it didn't fit the cultural and religious values of the day.

Wow! We've come a long way! We've seen how this one verse, "Deny yourself, take up your cross and follow me" when taken out of its context, seems to be about how we are to relate to others, but when understood *in* context, it's actually about something entirely different. It's Jesus' command, admonition, warning, even, to deny our false self—and all the voices and values that keep us trapped in that space—and live out of our true self, our soul self, our created-in-the-image-of-God self. May it be so. Amen and amen.

· · ·

At the beginning of this chapter I shared Dr. Johanna Olson's statement: "You're born with your gender identity. It's an immutable characteristic and part of your core being. . . . Your gender identity is not a choice. The choice piece of it is the choice you make about how to live authentically."

In the Gospel of Matthew Jesus said, "Deny your [false] self, take up your cross and follow me. . . . What does it profit a person to gain the whole world, yet lose their own soul?"

Jesus and Dr. Johanna both say that all people have choices to make. It's good to know that the Bible supports all of us choosing to live according to our true selves, our authentic selves, our divinely created selves—despite what the world thinks of our choices.

part 4

HOPE AND AFFIRMATION

9

GENDER VARIANT INDIVIDUALS
IN THE BIBLE

For me, one of the wonderful things about the Bible is that no matter how many times I read it, I can always find something new there. Three years ago I saw some surprising new things about a few Bible characters through a one-person play called *Transfigurations: Transgressing Gender in the Bible*, written and performed by activist, playwright, and biblical scholar Peterson Toscano. The play's promotional piece had said that in *Transfigurations* Toscano unearths gender blending "Bible characters—those people who do not fit in the gender binary, and who in transgressing and transcending gender, find themselves at the center of some of the most important Bible stories."[1] I was intrigued!

JACOB

Much to my surprise, one of the first biblical characters Toscano considered was one of the three founding fathers of Israel, Jacob himself! As you may know, the ancient Israelites were descended from Abraham, Isaac, and Jacob. Through his wives, Leah and Rebecca, and their maidservants, Jacob became the father of the twelve sons from whom the twelve tribes of Israel arose. In fact, "Israel" was the name Jacob had been given after he wrestled with God one night as he was returning home and preparing to unite with his twin brother, Esau, from whom he had been estranged for many years (Gen. 29–32).

Prior to seeing *Transfigurations*, I had read the story of Jacob many, many times. I had even preached on it on numerous occasions! Nevertheless, when Toscano did his performance that evening, he brought out something about Jacob that I had never seen, even though it had been there all along. To tell Jacob's story, this brilliant actor changed into the garb of Jacob's manly, hairy twin, Esau—while on stage—all the time talking to his audience. As Toscano fed us the background of this story, he also changed his mannerisms as he changed his clothes. His gait and movements became thick and lumbering, like those of a linebacker. Finally, to complete his transfiguration into Esau, he deepened his voice and began to tell in a scoffing tone how Jacob was a smooth-skinned sissy—a mama's boy—always hanging out among the tents with the women and doing girly stuff, like cooking and making stew. "Esau" went on to explain how Joseph never liked hanging out with the other men and doing the manly things that he enjoyed, things like hunting and being out in the wide open spaces.

When I saw Jacob portrayed in this way, I was shocked! How had I never seen this before?! It was right there, plain as day, in Genesis 25.

[19]This is the account of the family line of Abraham's son Isaac.

Abraham became the father of Isaac, [20]and Isaac was forty years old when he married Rebekah.... [21]Isaac prayed to the LORD on behalf of his wife, because she was childless. The LORD answered his prayer, and his wife Rebekah became pregnant. ... [24]When the time came for her to give birth, there were twin boys in her womb. [25]The first to come out was red, and his whole body was like a hairy garment; so they named him Esau. [26]After this, his brother came out, with his hand grasping Esau's heel; so he was named Jacob....

[27]The boys grew up, and Esau became a skillful hunter, a man of the open country, while Jacob was content to stay at home

among the tents. [28]Isaac, who had a taste for wild game, loved Esau, but Rebekah loved Jacob.

[29]Once when Jacob was cooking some stew, Esau came in from the open country, famished. [30]He said to Jacob, "Quick, let me have some of that red stew! I'm famished!" . . .

[31]Jacob replied, "First sell me your birthright."

Later, in Genesis 27:11, Jacob describes his brother and himself this way: "my brother Esau is a hairy man, and I'm a man with smooth skin."

Does all of this mean that Jacob was effeminate, or gay, or some form of transgender? We cannot know for sure, because along with not using the twenty-first-century words we find under the transgender umbrella, the Bible, as it was originally written, also did not use historically modern words like gay, lesbian, or homosexual.[2] Consequently, while we cannot conclusively determine the Patriarch Jacob's gender identity or sexual orientation from the biblical accounts, I think it is accurate to say that, given his preference for women's work and for spending his days among the women of his tribe, he was definitely gender variant; Jacob did not conform to the cultural expectations of the men of his day.

Granted, Jacob did perform the manly duty of siring children. However, I know many gay and transgender individuals today who entered into heterosexual marriages and had children because this was a cultural expectation, just as it was in Jacob's day. Also, a careful reading of Genesis 29:31–30:24 reveals that Jacob's procreating had a lot to do with his wives' jealous attempts to win his favor—but it never says whether he was enjoying it! Here is an excerpt from Genesis 30 (verses 14–24) regarding the two sisters, Leah and Rachel (Jacob's wives), vying for Jacob's attentions and using mandrakes as an aphrodisiac.[3]

[14]During wheat harvest, Reuben went out into the fields and found some mandrake plants, which he brought to his mother

Leah. Rachel said to Leah, "Please give me some of your son's mandrakes."

[15]But she said to her, "Wasn't it enough that you took away my husband? Will you take my son's mandrakes too?"

"Very well," Rachel said, "he can sleep with you tonight in return for your son's mandrakes."

[16]So when Jacob came in from the fields that evening, Leah went out to meet him. "You must sleep with me," she said. "I have hired you with my son's mandrakes." So he slept with her that night.

[17]God listened to Leah, and she became pregnant and bore Jacob a fifth son.

[18]Then Leah said, "God has rewarded me for giving my servant to my husband." So she named him Issachar.

[19]Leah conceived again and bore Jacob a sixth son. [20]Then Leah said, "God has presented me with a precious gift. This time my husband will treat me with honor, because I have borne him six sons." So she named him Zebulun.

[21]Some time later she gave birth to a daughter and named her Dinah.

[22]Then God remembered Rachel; he listened to her and enabled her to conceive. [23]She became pregnant and gave birth to a son and said, "God has taken away my disgrace." [24]She named him Joseph, and said, "May the LORD add to me another son."

These verses give us a feel for the jealous rivalry that was a key factor in Jacob's siring duties. (To really get a feel for that rivalry, read the whole account from Genesis 29:31 to 30:24!) Verse 16, where Leah tells Jacob, "You must sleep with me tonight. I have hired you with my son's mandrakes," makes Jacob sound like little more than a stud horse for hire!

In summary, we *do* know that Jacob fathered many children. What we do not know for sure is whether he did it out of culturally expected duty or heterosexual, cisgender desire. All we know for sure is that he was smooth skinned and liked to stay at home among the tents doing women's work, and that he was his mother's favorite. Meanwhile his hairy twin brother Esau, who loved to hunt and be out in the open country, was his father's favorite. There is definitely some gender variance going on here with Jacob, but it is hard to know how this variance would be classified using today's definitions.

Meanwhile, what *I personally knew for sure*, after being surprised by Toscano's eye-opening portrayal of Jacob, was that I had been reading the Bible through an incredibly thick heterosexual and cisgender lens—without even realizing that I was viewing things from this perspective! That is the only explanation I can think of for how I was able to read and preach on Jacob's story so many times without even noticing the gender variance that is so clearly present.

JOSEPH

The story of Joseph, one of Jacob's twelve sons, was also recounted by Toscano in *Transfigurations*. In fact, Joseph is such an interesting character that he has also been the subject of several movies and the hit musical *Joseph and the Amazing Technicolor Dreamcoat*.

In Genesis 37–47 we find the story of how Joseph's father, Jacob, gave him a wonderful robe, which made all his brothers hate him. Jacob's brothers also despised him because he told them about two of his dreams, which indicated that they would bow down to him and he would rule over them. In fact, Joseph's brothers hated him so much that they sold him to a caravan heading to Egypt. There, Potiphar, one of the royal guards, bought him to be a servant. All went well until Joseph, who was really good looking (scripture tells us that several times), started having to fend off the seductions of Potiphar's wife. During one of these rejections of his boss's wife, she claimed that Joseph attacked her, which got him thrown in prison. While in prison, he correctly interpreted the dreams of some of his fellow inmates, one of whom eventually recommended him to Pharaoh when the ruler was having some disturbing dreams. After correctly interpreting Pharaoh's dreams, Joseph became one of his most trusted advisors. Years later, during a time of widespread famine, ten of Joseph's brothers went down to Egypt seeking help. They met with Joseph in person, though not one of them recognized him! After testing his brothers in several ways, Joseph finally revealed himself to them and then forgave them for selling him to a caravan heading down to Egypt when he was young.

A California girl, after learning all this about Joseph, exclaimed, "Isn't it obvious? Joseph was like, so *gay*! I mean, he's got this fabulous rainbow colored coat, everyone comments on how cute he is, and he refuses to sleep with that Egyptian hottie! He's totally gay![4]

That might be the case. In fact, Bible commentators as far back as medieval times were noting that there was something different about Joseph.[5] Or could it be that Joseph was gender nonconforming?

This was the surprising insight into Joseph's story that Peterson Toscano offered in *Transfigurations*. He and other biblical scholars base their interpretation on key words found in this story in the thirty-seventh chapter of Genesis.[6] I have put this word in italics because it is significant.

> [2]This is the account of Jacob's family line. Joseph, a young man of seventeen, was tending the flocks with his brothers . . .
>
> [3]Now Israel loved Joseph more than any of his other sons, because he had been born to him in his old age; and he made *an ornate robe* for him. When his brothers saw that their father loved him more than any of them, they hated him and could not speak a kind word to him. . . .
>
> [23]So when Joseph came to his brothers [who had been out in the fields tending their flocks] they stripped him of his robe— the *ornate robe* he was wearing—[24]and they took him and threw him into the cistern. The cistern was empty; there was no water in it. . . .

> [28]So when . . . Midianite merchants came by, his brothers pulled Joseph up out of the cistern and sold him for twenty shekels of silver to the Ishmaelites, who took him to Egypt.
>
> [31]Then they got Joseph's robe, slaughtered a goat and dipped the robe in the blood. They took the *ornate robe* back to their father and said, "We found this. Examine it to see whether it is your son's robe."
>
> [33]He recognized it and said, "It is my son's robe! Some ferocious animal has devoured him. Joseph has surely been torn to pieces."
>
> [34]Then Jacob tore his clothes, put on sackcloth and mourned for his son many days."

As you can see, in Joseph's story there is a great deal of focus on this *ornate robe* that his father gave him. In the original Hebrew, the words translated here as "ornate robe" are *ketonet passim*. After his surprising telling of Joseph's story, Toscano shared a common guideline for biblical translation, one I had learned in seminary and that we have previously discussed in chapter 5. That guideline states that when you come across an uncommon word, you should look at how the same word is used in other places to help determine its meaning.

The phrase *ketonet passim* is uncommon in that it is used only five times in scripture; three of those occurrences are here in Joseph's story, and the other two are found in the thirteenth chapter of 2 Samuel, in a violent story about Princess Tamar, the daughter of King David. In Tamar's story there is a very clear statement about what a *ketonet passim* is, a statement that appears within the biblical text itself. (I have added italics for emphasis.) After Princess Tamar is raped by her brother Amnon,

> [17]He called his personal servant and said, "Get this woman out of my sight and bolt the door after her." [18]So his servant put

her out and bolted the door after her. She was wearing an *ornate robe, for this was the kind of garment the virgin daughters of the king wore.* [19]Tamar put ashes on her head and tore the *ornate robe* she was wearing. She put her hands on her head and went away, weeping aloud as she went.

Now why would a father who loves his son very much give him the kind of garment worn by the virgin daughters of kings? Wouldn't Jacob have known that wearing girls' clothing would make his beloved son a target of ridicule and bullying? And why would Joseph wear such a thing out in public? Wouldn't he have been embarrassed to be seen wearing a girls' garment? In *Transfigurations* Toscano stated that we do not know why the patriarch Jacob—the gender variant mama's boy who liked to cook and spend his time among the tents with the women—gave his son a female garment. One possible interpretation is that he was sympathetic to a boy who felt drawn to female activities and clothing. So out of his great love for his son Joseph, Jacob gave him an ornate robe that affirmed Joseph's gender nonconformity. Jacob knowingly and lovingly gave Joseph *the kind of garment worn by the virgin daughters of the king.* And Joseph wore this girly garment gladly.

As I sat through Toscano's brilliant performance of *Transfigurations* I was amazed to learn that Joseph's "coat of many colors" was actually the kind of garment worn by princesses! That put a totally different spin on this story! I was also startled to realize that Joseph being gender variant would explain the mystery of why his brothers hated him so very much. Think about it . . . many of us who have a sibling have experienced feelings of sibling rivalry, but most of us have never found a way to get rid of our sibling and then hatched a story to prove to our parents that he or she was dead! That sort of action goes *way beyond* typical feelings of sibling rivalry! However, if Joseph was his father's favorite and went around boasting that his brothers would one day bow down to him, *and* was gender nonconforming, then the intensity of his brothers' loathing makes a lot more sense. After all, many gender variant individuals are victims of violence today, and/or are rejected by their families and treated as though they were dead. Toscano inspired this line of thinking in my mind when he shared with his audience,

> Yes, the brothers use the torn and bloodied garment as a ruse to trick their father about what happened to Joseph. But if it was such a fine garment that they were envious over, they would have ditched their brother and one of them would have come home wearing the coat! Either that or they would have sold it and gotten a pretty penny for it. But there was something transgressive about the garment, and there was something punitive about their violence, as if they were saying, "We are going to teach you a lesson." This violence reminds me so much of the extreme violence I hear about today towards gender nonconforming people, particularly transgender people, especially transgender women of color.[7]

The possibility that Joseph was gender nonconforming could also explain another puzzling aspect of Joseph's story. It has always struck me as odd that not even one of Joseph's ten brothers recognized him when they went down to Egypt, seeking help because of the famine. Granted, it had been about twenty-two years since they had all seen each other.[8] However, don't you think you would recognize *something* about your sibling, even if their physical appearance had changed a great deal? Wouldn't you recognize their voice or some mannerism? Wouldn't something about that person put you in mind of the sibling you had once known? Unless, of course, your sibling was gender variant, and during the twenty-two years since you had last seen them they had worked at changing their voice and their mannerisms along with their appearance in order to more accurately present on the outside the person they knew themselves to be on the inside. The heavy cosmetics worn by both Egyptian men and women would have helped Joseph greatly in this process of feminizing his look.[9]

Now, I get that as human beings we often do not see what we are not expecting to see—and Joseph's brothers were certainly not expecting Pharaoh's top advisor to be the sibling they had sold to a caravan heading to Egypt some twenty years ago! Yet, I still have to wonder about this total lack of recognition by ten different people. Toscano's insightful interpretation, that Joseph was gender nonconforming, would certainly solve this mystery, just as it explains why Joseph's loving father would give him a garment worn by princesses, why Joseph would wear that girly garment so gladly, *and* why his brothers loathed him to the point of getting rid of him and telling their father he was dead.

DEBORAH

After portraying Esau's take on the gender variant nature of Jacob and Joseph, significant figures in Israel's history, Toscano turned his *Transfigurations* audience's attention to a lesser known biblical character, Deborah. We find Deborah's story in the book of Judges. This book contains the stories of the judges who led Israel after the death of Joshua (who had led the people into the Promised Land) but before the rise of Samuel and the eventual establishment of kings as the rulers of Israel. Deborah carried out the typical responsibilities of a judge during this time period: she heard and settled individual's disputes, she carried out the prophetic role of speaking to the people on God's behalf, and she was a military leader. Deborah's story is found in Judges 4–5.

> [4]Now Deborah, a prophet, the wife of Lappidoth, was leading Israel at that time. [5]She held court under the Palm of Deborah between Ramah and Bethel in the hill country of Ephraim, and the Israelites went up to her to have their disputes decided. [6]She sent for Barak son of Abinoam from Kedesh in Naphtali and said to him, "The LORD, the God of Israel, commands you: 'Go, take with you ten thousand men of Naphtali and Zebulun and lead them up to Mount Tabor. [7]I will lead Sisera, the commander of Jabin's army, with his chariots and his troops to the

Kishon River and give him into your hands.'" [*Author's note: According to Judges 4:3, Jabin, king of Canaan, had oppressed the Israelites for twenty years.*]

⁸Barak said to her, "If you go with me, I will go; but if you don't go with me, I won't go."

⁹"Certainly I will go with you," said Deborah. "But because of the course you are taking, the honor will not be yours, for the LORD will deliver Sisera into the hands of a woman." So Deborah went with Barak to Kedesh. ¹⁰There Barak summoned Zebulun and Naphtali, and ten thousand men went up under his command. Deborah also went up with him.

To summarize the ending of this story, Barak's troops were victorious that day. They soundly defeated King Jabin's army. Sisera, the army's commander, fled on foot when his troops were routed and took shelter in the tent of a foreign woman named Jael. While he was sleeping in her tent, that woman, in another very gender nonconforming act, drove a tent peg through Sisera's head and killed him. (If you're a fan of action flicks, then you have to love these Old Testament stories—lots of blood and violence!)

Living when we do—during an era when Margaret Thatcher has been prime minister of England, three of the judges serving on the U.S. Supreme Court are women, and Hillary Clinton is running for president—we may read this story of Deborah and think nothing of it. However, given the realities of the patriarchal time and era during which Deborah served as a judge in Israel, this account is nothing short of a gender variant miracle story!

These things that Deborah was doing—settling disputes, speaking on God's behalf, leading an army—these were all strictly men's work. In Deborah's day and age, women were basically nothing more than property. We have seen from Rachel and Leah's desperate rivalry and race to get pregnant that a woman's worth was measured by the number of children, and especially the number of sons, she bore to her husband. According to ancient Jewish law, contact with blood made a person ritually unclean, so not only were women ritually unclean for several days during their monthly menstrual cycle, but anyone who came in contact with them also became ritually unclean.

Living in a male-dominated culture such as this, what was it about Deborah that allowed her to even imagine that she could be a judge in Israel? Obviously, she must have had a different sense of herself than most of the women of her day. What was it about her that made men seek her out to settle their disputes? What qualities and characteristics did she possess that caused the military commander Barak to say, "If you go with me, I will go; but if you don't go with me, I won't go"? Apparently Deborah possessed a gender variant essence, a gender nonconforming energy that enabled herself and others to see and accept her in the masculine roles of judge, prophet, and military leader.

As I watched Toscano's portrayal of Deborah, again I marveled at the fact that, because I had always read scripture through a cisnormative lens (a perspective that assumes the norm to be that all persons are either strictly male or female), I had never stopped to consider how truly radical Deborah's gender nonconforming actions were. Nor had I considered what those actions might indicate about her gender identity. Toscano helped me to see that, like Jacob and Joseph, Deborah was definitely gender variant. As promised in the promotional piece for *Transfigurations*, this playwright/actor/activist had brilliantly revealed "Bible characters—who do not fit in the gender binary and who, in transgressing and transcending gender, find themselves at the center of some of the most important Bible stories."

HEGAI, EBED-MELECH, AND THE ETHIOPIAN EUNUCH

As previously discussed in chapter 3, eunuchs were the main category of gender variant individuals in the Bible. In *Transfigurations* Toscano noted that they were also key players in a number of Bible stories. For example, Hegai was the eunuch in charge of the palace women during the reign of Xerxes, king of Persia. Hegai played a major role in helping the Jewish girl, Esther, become Xerxes' new queen. This put her in a position to eventually save the Jewish people from an edict calling for their destruction. This story, found in the biblical book of Esther, is the basis of the Purim festival celebrated by Jewish people to this day.

In chapter 3 we noted the significance of the fact that the baptism of the Ethiopian eunuch in Acts 8 fulfills the prophecy from Isaiah 56, that God would give the formerly excluded eunuchs and foreigners a place in God's assembly. Toscano noted that a lesser known Ethiopian eunuch, Ebed-Melech, plays a key role in the prophet Jeremiah's story. Jeremiah 38 tells how Jeremiah had been thrown into a cistern and left to die because he had been delivering God's message that Jerusalem would fall to the Babylonians. However, Ebed-Melech told the king what had happened to Jeremiah and received permission to take thirty men and mount a rescue operation, thus saving the prophet's life.

Ebed-Melech, Hegai, the Ethiopian eunuch, Deborah, Joseph, and Jacob are all examples of gender variant individuals in the Scriptures. Yet I had never seen them until three years ago, when I had the privilege of seeing Peterson Toscana's eye opening play. That's what I love about the Bible; even having earned a seminary degree and spending years poring over its contents preparing sermons and Bible studies, I am still finding new things in this amazing book. I also love that the Bible is a place where *all* of us—gender conforming and gender variant alike—can find our stories being told—accounts of people just like us, stories that give us role models and hope and courage in the midst of our everyday lives.

· · ·

To learn more about Peterson Toscano, all of his plays, and his performance schedule, visit his website at www.PetersonToscano.com. If he's performing near where you live, do yourself a favor and *go*! If he has no plans to be in your area, consider joining with churches, seminaries, or other organizations to invite him to come and perform in your city.

10

JOHN 9 AND THE GIFTS GENDER VARIANT PEOPLE BRING TO THE WORLD

In the ninth chapter of John's Gospel we find a story about what happens when Jesus heals a man who has experienced visual impairment since birth.

> As he went along, he saw a man blind from birth. ²His disciples asked him, "Rabbi, who sinned, this man or his parents, that he was born blind?"
>
> ³"Neither this man nor his parents sinned," said Jesus, "but this happened so that the works of God might be displayed in him. ⁴As long as it is day, we must do the works of him who sent me. Night is coming, when no one can work. ⁵While I am in the world, I am the light of the world."
>
> ⁶After saying this, he spit on the ground, made some mud with the saliva, and put it on the man's eyes. ⁷"Go," he told him, "wash in the Pool of Siloam" (this word means "Sent"). So the man went and washed, and came home seeing.
>
> ⁸His neighbors and those who had formerly seen him begging asked, "Isn't this the same man who used to sit and beg?" ⁹Some claimed that he was.

Others said, "No, he only looks like him."

But he himself insisted, "I am the man."

[10]"How then were your eyes opened?" they asked.

[11]He replied, "The man they call Jesus made some mud and put it on my eyes. He told me to go to Siloam and wash. So I went and washed, and then I could see."

[12]"Where is this man?" they asked him.

"I don't know," he said.

[13]They brought to the Pharisees the man who had been blind. [14]Now the day on which Jesus had made the mud and opened the man's eyes was a Sabbath. [15]Therefore the Pharisees also asked him how he had received his sight. "He put mud on my eyes," the man replied, "and I washed, and now I see."

[16]Some of the Pharisees said, "This man is not from God, for he does not keep the Sabbath."

But others asked, "How can a sinner perform such signs?" So they were divided.

[17]Then they turned again to the blind man, "What have you to say about him? It was your eyes he opened."

The man replied, "He is a prophet."

[18]They still did not believe that he had been blind and had received his sight until they sent for the man's parents. [19]"Is this your son?" they asked. "Is this the one you say was born blind? How is it that now he can see?"

[20]"We know he is our son," the parents answered, "and we know he was born blind. [21]But how he can see now, or who opened his eyes, we don't know. Ask him. He is of age; he will speak for himself." [22]His parents said this because they were afraid of the Jewish leaders, who already had decided that anyone who acknowledged that Jesus was the Messiah would be

put out of the synagogue. [23]That was why his parents said, "He is of age; ask him."

[24]A second time they summoned the man who had been blind. "Give glory to God by telling the truth," they said. "We know this man is a sinner."

[25]He replied, "Whether he is a sinner or not, I don't know. One thing I do know. I was blind but now I see!"

[26]Then they asked him, "What did he do to you? How did he open your eyes?"

[27]He answered, "I have told you already and you did not listen. Why do you want to hear it again? Do you want to become his disciples too?"

[28]Then they hurled insults at him and said, "You are this fellow's disciple! We are disciples of Moses! [29]We know that God spoke to Moses, but as for this fellow, we don't even know where he comes from."

[30]The man answered, "Now that is remarkable! You don't know where he comes from, yet he opened my eyes. [31]We know that God does not listen to sinners. He listens to the godly person who does his will. [32]Nobody has ever heard of opening the eyes of a man born blind. [33]If this man were not from God, he could do nothing."

[34]To this they replied, "You were steeped in sin at birth; how dare you lecture us!" And they threw him out.

[35]Jesus heard that they had thrown him out, and when he found him, he said, "Do you believe in the Son of Man?"

[36]"Who is he, sir?" the man asked. "Tell me so that I may believe in him."

[37]Jesus said, "You have now seen him; in fact, he is the one speaking with you."

[38]Then the man said, "Lord, I believe," and he worshiped him.

[39]Jesus said, "For judgment I have come into this world, so that the blind will see and those who see will become blind."

[40]Some Pharisees who were with him heard him say this and asked, "What? Are we blind too?"

[41]Jesus said, "If you were blind, you would not be guilty of sin; but now that you claim you can see, your guilt remains."

One evening I was leading our church's support group for gender variant persons in a discussion of this story. I distinctly remember feeling the Holy Spirit fall upon those gathered as they realized that this man's parents had done the same thing to him that many of their parents had done. When living their divinely created, gender variant truth had forced their parents to make a choice between loving their children or losing their standing in their churches and communities, many parents had chosen to save their reputations and had turned their backs on their adult children. A hushed silence fell over the room as each person struggled with the mixed emotions brought on by their experience of the story—comfort in knowing that a biblical character who had found favor with Christ had experienced something similar to their experience, and the heartbreak of being reminded that they were still bearing the heavy cross of being rejected by their parents. Likewise, their interactions with those who had known them in the past were similar to this man's experiences. Some of their old friends and neighbors still recognize and acknowledge them; others do not.

Exploring this biblical story with a group of gender variant individuals was the most powerful experience I have ever had with this chapter from John's Gospel, although I have used it with many groups. So I would like to end our time together by considering the verses from the very beginning of this story. Jesus responded to his disciples' question "Rabbi, who sinned, this man or his parents, that he was born blind?" by saying, "Neither this man nor his parents sinned, but this happened so that the works of God might be displayed in him."

In what ways might "the works of God" be displayed in and through gender variant persons? To ask this question another way, what gifts do gender variant people bring to the body of Christ and to the world? Out of the many possible answers to these questions, I offer just a few, based on my personal experiences.

I saw my gender variant congregants bring a wonderful variety of gifts to our church's ministries. One used her gift of gregariousness very effectively as our head greeter. Several trans women played on our softball team, and one served as assistant coach, enabling our team to become an example, in the local women's softball league, of the radically inclusive nature of the body of Christ. A trans man used his considerable administrative gifts as vice-moderator of the church's board of directors. A trans woman graciously facilitated a book group for gender variant individuals. We had two musically talented cross-dressing congregants who often provided special music for worship. Several trans women were soloists in our choir and one directed our singers for a while. A gender fluid congregant was a faithful volunteer at our Wednesday night dinners for the homeless. And it's hard to say where the church would be without the many and varied gifts our transgender office manager and sexton brings to her work.

Likewise, I know gender variant individuals who bring a vast array of skills and talents to our world, serving as ministers, writers, lawyers, community organizers, IT specialists, educators, EMTs, engineers, journalists, therapists, corporate trainers, and government employees.

On a personal note, I am grateful for the gifts of honesty and courage I have seen manifested by gender variant people. They have inspired me to be as honest as they are about who God has created me to be, challenging me to ask myself, "Who am I vocationally? What are my unique, God-given gifts, aptitudes, and interests? Am I honoring and using them to their fullest? Who am I spiritually? What sort of spiritual practices work best for me, given my divinely created temperament and proclivities?"

Next, gender variant friends and congregants inspire me to live my answers to the preceding questions as courageously as they live their truths. Let's face it, all of us are subjected to peer, parental, familial, societal, and even religious expectations about how we are and are not supposed to act. So to act in ways that are true to who we are but that may be contrary to people's expectations of us takes great courage—for all of us! Watching transgender people courageously live their lives has been a huge inspiration to me to exercise the courage I need to live my divinely created truth each and every day.

Given the ways that gender variant people inspire me daily, and all the gifts I have seen them bring to the church and to the world, I close with two prayers.

My prayer for all gender variant people is that you will let the light of your vast and varied gifts continue to shine brightly. My prayer for all nontransgender people is that, in the same way we delight in the dusk and dawn of each new day, may we also celebrate the dusk/dawn light of gender variant individuals and the many gifts they bring to the church and to the world.

APPENDIX A

How to Make your Congregation or Group Trans Friendly

These suggestions are designed to be used by congregants, church leaders, and staff members; pastors; professors; students in Christian campus organizations; and chaplains in various settings.

1. Educate your leaders and constituents about gender variance in children, youth, and adults.

While there are many good books on these topics, here are several reliable websites with good, basic information that can be accessed and read quickly and easily. A group or team of leaders could spend just ten minutes at the start of their meetings over several months reading and discussing this information to begin educating themselves.

- Begin by familiarizing yourselves with the language of transgender culture, including the correct use of pronouns. See www.glaad.org/reference/transgender and www.transequality .org/issues/resources/transgender-terminology.
- Understand the various dimensions of gender and sexuality. See itspronouncedmetrosexual.com/2012/01/the-genderbread-person.
- Learn about the transgender experience at www.transequality.org/issues/resources/understanding-trans gender and also at www.apa.org/topics/lgbt/transgender.aspx.
- Learn about cross-dressers: www.tri-ess.org/.
- Learn about intersex people: www.apa.org/topics/lgbt/ intersex.aspx.

- Learn about transgender children and youth: www.chla.org/blog /physicians-and-clinicians/transgender-community-questions-answers-johanna-olson-md-%E2%80%93-chla%E2%80%99s.

- See "Topics for exploration" scattered throughout "Appendix B: Discussion Guide" for suggestions of other topics and YouTube videos that are highly educational.

- Invite gender variant people to do training.

- Because many gender variant individuals are children or youth, it will be especially important for a congregation to educate its Sunday school staff, youth group leaders, *and* youth group members about the transgender experience so *all* can be welcoming of gender variant individuals.

2. Educate your leaders and constituents regarding what the Bible says about gender variance.

- Use the discussion guide in appendix B to lead a four- or five-week Bible study or discussion group or to facilitate a one-time discussion after participants have read the whole book.

- Offer a sermon series on gender variance.

- Invite transgender clergy and/or the author to come preach or do a presentation. Contact the author at www.Transformation JourneysWW.com.

- Invite Peterson Toscano to come to your church, city, or campus to perform *Transfigurations* and to speak to various groups. Contact Peterson at https://petersontoscano.com/.

- If your congregation or group includes people from highly diverse theological backgrounds, you may want to read, at least for your own personal knowledge, Mark Yarhouse's *Understanding Gender Dysphoria: Navigating Transgender Issues in a Changing Culture*, a Christian Association for Psychological Studies book. Yarhouse, a clinical psychologist with a private practice, is a highly respected researcher and academician. He writes from an evangelical viewpoint and gives a comprehensive and pastoral overview of the various Christian perspectives on the transgender experience. Yarhouse's book is much longer and more academic/research oriented than this book, so please give careful consideration to whether or not it would be helpful to your constituents. It also leans toward seeing gender variance as a result of the Fall of humanity instead of seeing it as an expression of God's good and diverse creation.

3. Be proactive in reaching out to gender variant individuals and their loved ones.

- Provide meeting space for gender variant support groups and family support groups, such as PFLAG. (Even though the acronym PFLAG technically stands for "Parents, Families, and Friends of Lesbians and Gays," PFLAG groups also attract the friends and family members of gender variant individuals.)

- In all media sources where you indicate whom you welcome, be sure to include the phrase "persons of all gender identities and expressions." Saying that you welcome LGBT persons or persons of all sexual orientations does not necessarily let gender variant individuals know whether *they* are welcome too. You have to be explicit.

- Make sure sermons and book or Bible studies on gender variance are advertised where people in the community (not just those who are members of your congregation or group) will see them—on your church or chapel marquee, in local LGBTQI publications, on the bulletin board at local coffee shops, and supermarkets, etc.

- Research counseling centers in your area that specifically offer services to the transgender community and let them know that your congregation or group is trans welcoming. Also send them news of upcoming trans-related events you are hosting.

- If there is a chapter of Tri-Ess in your area, contact them to let them know that you welcome cross-dressers and to extend a special invitation to any gender variant related events you have planned.

- Reach out to your local LGBTQI community center to let them know you are trans friendly and be sure to send them fliers to post about upcoming trans-related events.

- Host an educational event, like a panel discussion and/or a movie night, to help the wider community learn about gender variant issues.

- Collaborate with your local Pride Organization to host events during Pride Month. Put a float in the annual Pride parade and/or sponsor a booth at a Pride festival.

- Find more points of contact with transgender groups and services through the GLBT National Resource Database at www.glbtnearme.org.

4. Offer a warm, welcoming environment when gender variant people and/or their loved ones show up.

- Say "Hello!" and engage in conversation, just as you would with any newcomer(s). This may sound "obvious" or like no big deal, but it could mean a great deal to gender variant guests and/or their family and friends.

- Use the pronouns that match the person's name presentation. If you cannot tell which pronoun to use, simply ask. Most gender variant people are happy to clarify, partly because the question shows you have a sensitivity to and respect for gender matters. As a refresher, see www.glaad.org/reference/transgender.

- Encourage the pastor or chaplain to include gender variant people and their experiences in sermon illustrations and even as sermon topics. (See the sermon in chapter 8, the story about John

9 in chapter 10, and the sermon at www.friends-ucc.org/index
.php/new-sermon-page/sermon/98-the-princess-dress-and-
the-name-of-jesus as examples.)

- Provide at least a few gender-neutral restrooms for all people.
  These can be helpful, not only to gender variant congregants,
  but also to those who may need to provide restroom assistance
  to young children, elderly persons, or differently abled loved
  ones.

- Be intentional about including gender variant individuals in
  opportunities for service and positions of leadership. Many have
  experienced cultural discrimination, even to the point of being
  ostracized by family and friends. Consequently, some gender
  variant folks may need to be personally invited to use their
  unique gifts and talents in service to the body of Christ. They
  may not readily respond to general calls for volunteers.

APPENDIX B

Discussion Guide

NOTES TO GROUP LEADER

This book lends itself very well to a four- to five-week Bible study or book discussion group, requiring that participants read about twenty to twenty-five pages per week. If using a four-week format, I recommend asking group members to commit to reading the introduction and chapters 1–3 before the first gathering, so they will come ready to discuss. Cover chapters 4–6 during your second session. Chapter 7 can be the focus of your third gathering. End by discussing chapters 8–10 during your final session. If using a five-week format, I recommend the intro and chapters 1–2 for the first session, chapters 3–4 for the second session, chapters 5–6 for the third, chapter 7 for the fourth, and chapters 8–10 for the final session.

Depending on your group's demographics and interests, you may want to delegate some "Topics for Exploration" at the end of each session. Topics may arise out of that particular session, and I have also offered suggestions. Individuals can then be invited to briefly share what they learned with the group at the beginning of each session and/or to share more about their topic as it is discussed during your time together.

It could be helpful to open discussion of the book's first chapters with a consideration of the four continuums relating to biological gender, gender identity, gender expression, and sexual orientation represented in the "Genderbread Person" diagram found at http://itspronouncedmetrosexual.com/2012/01/the-genderbread-person. This is a link to the original version, which the creator has since updated more than once. You can access all versions from this link and decide from there which version would be most helpful to print off and discuss with your particular group.

I know I have given you more here than you can probably use in each session, so feel free to pick and choose those discussion questions that will work best for your group. May your discussions be deep and life-giving!

CHAPTER 1—WHAT WE ARE AND ARE NOT TALKING ABOUT: LGB AND TQI

Discussion Questions

1. Prior to reading this chapter, were you familiar with the distinctions between L, G, B, and T, Q, and I?

2. As a group, brainstorm the names of people you've heard or read about in the media who are lesbian, gay, bisexual, transgender, queer, questioning, and intersex. Can you think of at least one person in each category? If not, why might you not have heard about this type of individual?

CHAPTER 2—CULTURAL CONTEXT: NOW AND THEN

Discussion Questions

1. Have any of you seen some of the TV programs featuring fictional transgender (transsexual) characters—such as *Glee, Orange Is the New Black, Trans-Parent, Sense8, The Bold and the Beautiful*—or reality shows featuring trans individuals— *Becoming Us, I Am Cait, I Am Jazz,* and two seasons of *America's Next Top Model?* Discuss your impressions of these characters and/or individuals.

2. Do you remember a time or incident in your childhood when you first became aware of your gender? What did you think and feel about gender at that point?

3. Have you ever had an experience of knowing yourself to be different from who others thought you were or wanted you to be? (Maybe your parents or significant other wanted you to choose one career, but you wanted to pursue another. Perhaps your church held to a certain belief, but you believed differently.) Talk about your own experience of not fitting in to cultural expectations.

4. Why do you think trans people are willing to risk losing their family, friends, faith communities, jobs, and places to live in order to transition and live according to their internal gender identity?

   Have you ever lost any of these things: a friend, your job, housing, your parent's approval, church membership, etc.? What sort of impact did that have on your life?

   What might trans people experience (physically, emotionally, financially, spiritually) as a result of facing all or some of these losses?

5. Transgender (transsexual) people feel their gender identity does not match the gender they were assigned at birth, so most desire to live full-time as the gender with which they identify (in so far as it is possible for them). Cross-dressers *are* comfortable with the gender they were assigned at birth, but they also have a *need* to spend some time dressed and presenting as the opposite sex. Discuss whether it's easier for you to understand/get/relate to the experiences of transsexuals or cross-dressers.

6. Discuss any questions or comments group members have about others under the transgender umbrella: persons who are intersex, genderqueer, bigender, two-spirit, etc.

Topics for exploration in preparation for discussion in the second session:
- Find out what's required in your state to change the gender marker on your driver's license.

- Find out the cost of "top surgery" (breast augmentation or reduction) or "bottom surgery" (genital reconstruction—collectively these surgeries are known as "gender confirmation surgery") for both trans men and trans women.

- Learn more about transgender persons on the National Center for Transgender Equality's website at "Understanding Transgender People FAQ," www.transequality.org/issues/resources/understanding-transgender-people-faq.

- Learn more about transgender people on the American Psychological Association's (APA) website at "Answers to Your Questions About Transgender People, Gender Identity and Gender Expression," www.apa.org/topics/lgbt/transgender.aspx.

- On the APA website, also learn more about the impact of the societal challenges transgender people face in the article "Transgender Today" at www.apa.org/monitor/2013/04/transgender.aspx.

CHAPTER 3—VERSES ABOUT EUNUCHS: DEUTERONOMY 23:1, ISAIAH 56:1–7, ACTS 8:26–39

Discussion Questions

1. Discuss the differences and similarities between eunuchs in the Bible and gender variant people today.

2. Are you personally familiar with stories of Middle Eastern–looking people in the United States being harassed after 9/11 or as a result of the rise of ISIS today? Do you yourself have any friends or relatives who are immigrants or the children or grandchildren of immigrants who are being encouraged by family members to "marry their own kind"?

3. Do you agree or disagree with the author's suggestions that the "ancient Israelites may have been hearing God's word to them through the lens of their own fears, so they wrote that it was

God's will that they exclude others . . . a perspective God later corrected through Isaiah, Jesus, and the Acts of the Holy Spirit"? If you disagree, share your theory as to why we see this movement from exclusion to inclusion in the Bible.

4. The author writes: "The fact that the Bible itself shows a historical movement and shift in the Israelites' understanding of how God would have them relate to the gender variant people of their day suggests that God may also have an accepting, affirming, and inclusive attitude towards the gender variant people of our day." Given the differences and similarities that exist between the eunuchs of biblical times and gender variant people today, in what ways do you think the biblical movement towards inclusion of eunuchs should or should not inform the church's modern-day relationship with gender variant people?

CHAPTER 4—LEVITICUS 21 AND HOLINESS

Discussion Questions

1. The author writes: "The reason the church no longer uses this passage as part of its requirements for ordination is because the New Testament reveals that, through Christ, the requirements of the Old Testament law have been fulfilled (see Acts 15, Galatians 3, Hebrews 8–10). Consequently, Christians no longer observe all the requirements of Old Testament law." Discuss examples of other Old Testament laws that Christians no longer follow.

2. Discuss other stories from the Gospels that demonstrate Jesus' teaching that it is not the things that people come in contact with on the outside that makes them unclean, impure, or unholy, but the thoughts and actions that arise from inside them.

3. Discuss and/or research where your denomination stands on the ordination of transgender people and why it takes that stance.

Topics for exploration in preparation for discussing chapters 5–6

- Learn more about cross-dressers at www.tri-ess.org.
- Learn more about intersex persons on the American Psychological Association's website at "Answers to Your Questions About Individuals With Intersex Conditions," www.apa.org/topics/lgbt/intersex.aspx.

CHAPTER 5—DEUTERONOMY 22:5: CROSS-DRESSING TO EXPRESS ONE'S TRUTH OR TO DO HARM?

Discussion Questions

1. In the beginning of this chapter the author suggests three guidelines for arriving at a responsible understanding of a Bible passage: (1) understanding the meaning of each of the words in their original languages, (2) understanding the passage within its historical/cultural context, and (3) understanding the passage within the context of the whole Bible.

   What guidelines do you use for interpreting scripture, especially verses that may seem contradictory to other scriptural teachings and/or to modern-day scientific findings or beliefs (for example, the modern belief that stoning people to death and killing adulterers, as directed in Deut. 22:21–22, is not a good idea)?

2. At the end of the section "Interpretations Based on the Meanings of Words and Immediate Context," the author offers four different ways that commentators have interpreted Deuteronomy 22:5 based on word meanings and context. Discuss the pros and cons of each of these interpretations. Which interpretation seems most reasonable to you and why?

3. The author indicates that even if Deuteronomy 22:5 were a prohibition against cross-dressing as we know it today we should no longer be concerned about it since Jesus came to fulfill the Old Testament law, so Christians are no longer bound by it, and

since we do not follow any of the other laws found in that same chapter. Can you think of any reasons that people might offer for why such a prohibition *should* still be observed today? Which reasons are most compelling to you?

4. Based on what you have read in this chapter, do you think Deuteronomy 22:5 is addressing cross-dressing as it is practiced today, or do you think it is a prohibition against the ancient Israelites using the clothes of the opposite gender to disguise their true selves for deceptive purposes and/or for cultic practices?

5. Discuss your thoughts and feelings about the author's statement: "Since gender variant people today are cross-dressing in order *to* express their true selves, in order to *not* deceive others and so harm relationships, I believe this verse is actually an affirmation to gender variant people to dress in the clothing that best expresses their true gender identity."

CHAPTER 6—MATTHEW 19:11-12 AND WHAT JESUS HAD TO SAY ABOUT GENDER VARIANCE

Discussion Questions

1. The author suggests three things that Jesus might have meant when he said that some people are born eunuchs: that they are gay, transgender, or intersex. Discuss what you think Jesus meant by this.

2. Brainstorm some of the ways in which Jesus might have known that there were eunuchs who were born that way.

3. The author writes: "The fact that Jesus included the one thing the Gospels report him saying about gender variance in the very same conversation in which he quotes the verse about God creating humans male and female (Gen. 1:27) indicates that Jesus was well aware that there were more than just two ways to live out one's gender—that male and female were not the only two realities." Do you agree that Jesus' inclusion of what he said

about eunuchs in this discussion indicates his belief that there are more than two ways to live out one's gender? Discuss.

4. Do you think that Christians should respond to the gender variant people of today with the same acceptance and lack of condemnation that Jesus exhibited regarding eunuchs, the gender variant people of his day? Why or why not?

5. Discuss some of the suggestions from Appendix A for creating a trans friendly congregation or fellowship group. Which would be the easiest to carry out in your context? Which would be the most challenging?

Topics for exploration in preparation for discussing chapter 7

- Bring in definitions and common examples of "merism" and examples of merism in the Bible.

- Google one of the most well-documented trans children in the United States, Jazz Jennings. You'll find lots out there about her. You might want to start with this video: www.youtube.com /watch?v=Jbg-LdVdNk0.

- Watch this YouTube video of a young transgender couple that aired on ABC's 20/20: www.youtube.com/watch?v=SNCJ6V f7qOM.

- Research transgender people across cultures worldwide. Do a general search on this topic and also specifically look up the Hiijra of India, the Fa'afafine of Samo, the Katoey of Thailand, the Muxe of Mexico, the Mahu of Hawaii, and Native American Two-Spirits.

CHAPTER 7—GENESIS 1:27 AND THE ARGUMENT FROM CREATION

Discussion Questions

1. What do you think about the author's perspective that Genesis 1 is a poetic account of the creation story and not a scientific explanation of how things came to be?

2. One definition of a merism is a figure of speech in which two contrasting things are used to indicate something in its entirety. A common example is the expression "I looked *high and low* for it," indicating that you looked everywhere. A merism might also use several parts of something to indicate the whole of it. An example of this usage is the phrase "lock, stock, and barrel," which uses several significant parts of a gun to indicate the totality of it or something else. In Psalm 139:1–3 the writer uses several merisms to indicate God's complete and total knowledge of the psalmist (italics added for emphasis).

> You have searched me, LORD,
> and you know me.
> You know *when I sit and when I rise*;
> you perceive my thoughts from afar.
> You discern *my going out and my lying down*;
> you are familiar with all my ways.

Do you think the writer of Genesis 1 might be using "night and day," "land and dry seas," "plants and animals," "male and female" as merisms, as figures of speech in which two contrasting things are used to express the entirety of something?

3. The author argues that the existence of intersex people indicates that God does create more than just male and female. Do you think this is a valid argument? Why or why not?

4. Discuss whether you think gender variance occurs as a result of "the Fall" or as a result of God's good and diverse creation.

Imagine living your whole life in a culture that says that some aspect of your being that you did not choose and that you cannot change (perhaps your eye color or your height) is evidence of the Fall. Imagine that this immutable aspect of yourself is seen as a disability, as less than the best God intends. Discuss how this might make you feel about that aspect of yourself and/or about yourself in general.

5. The author suggests that our culture, in general, does *not* operate under the assumption that our bodies are somehow more indicative of who we are than does our personality/mind/spirit/soul. Can you think of examples, beyond the ones the author gives, that support or challenge this perspective?

6. Why do you think our society is accepting of a genetic woman who gets breast implants but often disapproving of a trans woman who does the same? Why is our culture more approving of a genetic man who wants to get a hair transplant to alleviate balding than it is of a trans man who wants to get a "masculine" haircut?

7. The 2011 study the author cites indicating that the attempted suicide rate for transgender people is 41 percent also showed that the national average suicide rate was 1.6 percent. What might the great disparity in these numbers indicate about the transgender experience? Discuss how God might see these numbers and what God might want us to do in response to them.

8. The author argues that the testimony of two-, three-, and four-year-old trans children, and of transgender adults who likewise sensed there was something different about their gender from similar early ages, is evidence that our internal sense of ourselves is a stronger and more valid determinant of our gender than are our genitals. We all know that it is not "good form" to define a word by using that word in its definition. Is relying on the testimony of trans children, youth, and adults to define what determines gender a bit like using that word in its definition when you're trying to define it? Should their testimony be considered in deciding what should determine gender? Why or why not?

9. Discuss the stories of the parents who had transgender children. Do you think there are other things they should have tried or done? What would you do if you had a three-year-old who was telling you that they were not the sex that matched their genitals? Did reading these stories about transgender children have a different impact on you than reading or hearing the stories of transgender adults?

10. The author gives numerous biblical examples of times when God has called God's people to embrace a new belief. Might it be as challenging for Christians to accept that gender variant people are a part of God's good creation as it was for the early Christians to accept that God no longer required them to keep kosher (Acts 10–11:18)? Discuss.

11. Were you aware that there are eleven different countries that offer an option other than male or female on their citizens' passports? What impact might allowing for a third gender option on American passports have on U.S. culture? If Jesus were a member of the U.S. Congress and this issue was to come before the House or Senate, WWJD? (What would Jesus do?)

Topics for exploration in preparation for discussing chapters 8–10

- Research transgender people throughout history.

- Learn about the proper way to address gender variant individuals at www.glaad.org/reference/transgender.

- Read one of the leading U.S. pediatrician's answers to questions about trans children and youth at www.chla.org/blog/physicians -and-clinicians/transgender-community-questions-answers-johanna-olson-md-%E2%80%93-chla%E2%80%99s.

- Watch that same pediatrician answer questions about trans children and youth in brief video clips at www.kidsinthehouse .com/expert/parenting-advice-from-johanna-olson-md.

- Read, listen to, or watch the sermon "The Princess Dress and the Name of Jesus" at www.friends-ucc.org/index.php/new-sermon-page/sermon/98-the-princess-dress-and-the-name-of-jesus.

CHAPTER 8—MATTHEW 16:13-27 AND THE NOTION OF "CHOICE"

Discussion Questions

1. Discuss Dr. Johanna Olson's perspective that gender identity is an immutable characteristic, a part of your core being and not a choice. Do you feel like your gender identity was a part of your core being or did you choose it?

2. Throughout this book the author has stressed the importance of looking at the biblical, historical, and cultural context of a passage in order to interpret it responsibly. Do you think this is an important criterion for understanding the Bible? What other criteria do you use to understand the Scriptures?

3. Prior to reading this chapter, had you usually interpreted Matthew 16:24, "deny yourself, take up your cross and follow me" to mean that you should sacrifice your own needs and heart's desires for God and for others? If not, how had you interpreted it?

4. What do you think of the author's interpretation that Matthew 16:24 "is not a passage about how we are to relate to others. This is Jesus' teaching about how we are to relate to our selves—to our false self, the self that has been indoctrinated with the values of this world, and our true self, our soul self—the self that is made in the image of God"?

5. Do you think it's appropriate for the author to compare what Rosa Parks did by refusing to move to the back of the bus, and what the author's college roommate did by choosing a career as a teacher instead of a doctor, with the choice a transgender person or a gay person makes to come out?

6. The author gave numerous examples of what it looked like in the lives of various people when they more fully embraced who God had created them to be. Are there any aspects of your divinely created truth that you feel God might be calling you to embrace more fully? How do you think your choice to live your life more authentically might be received by others?

CHAPTER 9—GENDER VARIANT INDIVIDUALS IN THE BIBLE

Discussion Questions

1. Discuss experiences each of you have had of hearing a very familiar Bible story in a fresh, new way.

2. Discuss the possibility that Jacob may have been gender variant, based on the biblical description of him as one who was content to stay at home among the tents, and that he cooked and was his mother's favorite. Given the rivalry between his wives, Rebecca and Leah, about having children, and the importance of childbearing in the culture of the ancient Israelites, what might the fact that Jacob sired the twelve sons who became the twelve tribes of Israel say about his possible gender variance?

3. Brainstorm possible reasons for why Jacob might have given his son Joseph a "princess dress," a *ketonet passim*.

4. The author suggests that understanding Joseph as a gender non-conforming person answers many questions regarding Joseph's story, such as why his father gave him a girl's garment, why Joseph would wear a girl's garment, why his brothers hated him enough to sell him into slavery and tell his father he was dead, and why not even one of those same brothers would recognize him some twenty years later. Do you agree with this perspective, or do you think there are other equally plausible explanations for these aspects of Joseph's story? Discuss.

5. The author writes that the reason she had never stopped to consider the radically gender variant nature of Deborah's role as a judge in Israel was because in the past she had read scripture through a cis-normative lens, that is, from a perspective that assumes the norm to be that all persons are either strictly male or female. Discuss whether you have also been reading Bible stories through a cis-normative lens and if this chapter has had any impact on that perspective.

CHAPTER 10—JOHN 9 AND THE GIFTS GENDER VARIANT PEOPLE BRING TO THE WORLD

Discussion Questions

1. The author shares how significant this story from John 9, of Jesus healing the man born blind, was for a group of transgender parishioners. Can you think of other Bible stories that might particularly resonate with gender variant individuals?

2. Discuss the gifts that gender variant people you know—either personally or through the media—bring to the body of Christ and to the world.

ENDNOTES

CHAPTER 1

1. "Transgender Terminology," National Center for Transgender Equality, January 15, 2014, accessed November 15, 2015, http://www.transequality.org/issues/resources/transgender-terminology.

CHAPTER 2

1. The phrase "the gender they were assigned at birth" is a more respectful way to speak of people's sex or gender, since transgender individuals feel that their gender is determined more by their internal sense of themselves than by their genitalia, and since intersex persons may be born with ambiguous genitalia or external genitalia that does not match their internal reproductive organs or their chromosomes.

2. For more good, basic information about trans people, see these sources: the "Understanding Transgender People FAQ" link on the National Center for Transgender Equality's website at http://www.transequality.org/issues/resources/understanding-transgender-people-faq and the "Answers to Your Questions About Transgender People, Gender Identity and Gender Expression" page on the American Psychological Association's website at http://www.apa.org/topics/lgbt/transgender.aspx, both accessed March 28, 2016.

3. Tri-Ess, the Society for the Second Self, accessed December 2, 2015, http://tri-ess.org.

4. "FAQ: Specific Conditions," Accord Alliance, accessed November 10, 2015, http://www.accordalliance.org/learn-about-dsd/faqs.

5. Georgiann Davis, e-mail message to author, April 21, 2016.

6. Georgiann Davis, "Wrestling with Privacy, Visibility, and Legitimacy," March 1, 2016, InterACT, Advocates for Intersex Youth, blog, accessed July 1, 2016, http://interactadvocates.org/wrestling-with-privacy-visibility-and-legitimacy/.

7. "Transgender Terminology," National Center for Transgender Equality, January 15, 2014, accessed November 15, 2015, http://www.transequality.org/issues/resources/transgender-terminology.

8. Aimee Lee Ball, "Who Are You on Facebook Now? Facebook Customizes Gender with 50 Different Choices," *New York Times*, April 4, 2014, accessed November 12, 2015, http://www.nytimes.com/2014/04/06/fashion/facebook-customizes-gender-with-50-different-choices.html?_r=0.

9. James Orr, general editor, "Entry for Eunuch," International Standard Bible Encyclopedia Online, accessed November 14, 2015, http://www.biblestudytools.com/dictionary/eunuch.

CHAPTER 4

1. "Leviticus—Introduction," *The Holy Bible, New International Version* (Grand Rapids, Zondervan, 1986), 154.

2. Matthew Maule, "Who are America's Transgender Clergy?" July 27, 2015, Juicy Ecumenism: The Institute on Religion & Democracy's Blog, accessed March 26, 2016, https://juicyecumenism.com/2015/07/27/who-are-americas-transgender-clergy.

CHAPTER 5

1. Theresa Scott, "My Thoughts on Transsexualism and Christian Theology," Happily Theresa's Place, blog, accessed December 4, 2015, http://theresas179.weebly.com/bible.html.

2. Justin Tanis, *Trans-Gendered: Theology, Ministry, and Communities of Faith* (Cleveland: Pilgrim Press, 2003), 63–66.

3. Lisa Edwards, "Cross-Dressing and Drag," Keshet, accessed March 15, 2015, http://www.keshetonline.org/transtexts/cross-dressing-and-drag.

4. Sandra Stewart, "Commentaries on Deuteronomy 22.5," The Gender Tree, accessed December 4, 2015, http://gendertree.com/Deuteronomy.htm.

5. Ibid.

CHAPTER 6

1. For personal stories of persons born with one type of intersex condition, Androgen Insensitivity Syndrome, go to the Member Stories page of the AIA-DSD Support Group (International support group for people with androgen insensitivity syndrome and related conditions) at http://aisdsd.org/who-we-are/member-stories/.

2. See the 2014 Southern Baptist Convention's resolution "On Transgender Identity" for an example of this perspective. http://www.sbc.net/resolutions/2250/on-transgender-identity.

CHAPTER 7

1. "Kingdom (biology)," Wikipedia, accessed November 29, 2015, https://en.wikipedia.org/wiki/Kingdom_(biology).

2. "Intersex," updated July 10, 2015, by Neil K. Kaneshiro, MD, Medline Plus, accessed November 30, 2015, https://www.nlm.nih.gov/medlineplus/ency/article/001669.htm.

3. "Answers to Your Questions About Individuals With Intersex Conditions," American Psychological Association, accessed November 28, 2015, http://www.apa.org/topics/lgbt/intersex.aspx.

4. "How Common is Intersex?" Intersex Society of North America, accessed November 29, 2015, http://www.isna.org/faq/frequency.

5. Melanie Blackless, Anthony Charuvastra, Amanda Derryck, Anne Fausto-Sterling, Karl Lauzanne, and Ellen Lee, 2000, "How sexually dimorphic are we? Review and synthesis." *American Journal of Human Biology* 12:151–66.

6. For an in-depth discussion of the American medical community's interaction with intersex persons see Georgiann Davis, *Contesting Intersex: The Dubious Diagnosis* (New York: NYU Press, 2015).

7. For a list of advocacy and support groups for intersex persons, click "Where can I find more information about intersex conditions?" on the "Answers to Your Questions About Individuals With Intersex Conditions" page of the American Psychological Association's website, http://www.apa.org/topics/lgbt/intersex.aspx.

8. For a well-articulated discussion of the three main Christian perspectives on gender variance, see the section "Different Frameworks for Conceptualizing Gender Identity Concerns" in chapter 2, "A Christian

Perspective on Gender Dysphoria," of Mark Yarhouse's book *Understanding Gender Dysphoria: Navigating Transgender Issues in a Changing Culture* (Downers Grove, IL: InterVarsity Press Academic, 2015).

9. "Answers to Your Questions about Transgender People, Gender Identity and Gender Expression," American Psychological Association, accessed December 15, 2015, http://www.apa.org/topics/lgbt/transgender.aspx.

10. "On Transgender Identity," 2014, Southern Baptist Convention, accessed December 15, 2015, http://www.sbc.net/resolutions/2250/on-transgender-identity.

11. "National Transgender Discrimination Survey: Executive Summary," National Center for Transgender Equality, September 11, 2012, accessed April 2, 2015, http://www.transequality.org/issues/resources/national-transgender-discrimination-survey-executive-summary.

12. Alan B. Goldberg and Joneil Adriano, "'I'm a Girl'—Understanding Transgender Children," April 27, 2007, ABC News, accessed December 17, 2015, http://abcnews.go.com/2020/story?id=3088298&page=1.

13. Ibid.

14. Marlo Mack, "Op-ed: Finally, Some Reliable Research on Trans Kids Like Mine," *The Advocate,* February 11, 2015, accessed December 15, 2015, http://www.advocate.com/commentary/2015/02/11/op-ed-finally-some-reliable-research-trans-kids-mine.

15. "Johanna Olson-Kennedy, MD," Children's Hospital Los Angeles, accessed December 15, 2015, http://www.chla.org/profile/johanna-olson-kennedy-md.

16. Gendermom, "Your Questions Answered," blog, October 12, 2015, accessed December 12, 2015, https://gendermom.wordpress.com/2015/10/12/your-questions-answered.

17. "Transgender Community Questions & Answers With Johanna Olson, MD–CHLA's Transyouth Program," April 23, 2015, Children's Hospital Los Angeles, blog, accessed December 15, 2015, http://www.chla.org/blog/physicians-and-clinicians/transgender-community-questions-answers-johanna-olson-md---chla's.

18. Aron Macarow, "These Eleven Countries are Way Ahead of the US on Trans Issues," attn:, February 9, 2015, accessed November 28, 2015, http://www.attn.com/stories/868/transgender-passport-status.

CHAPTER 8

1. Johanna Olson, "When parents don't support their transgendered child," video, 1:02, accessed February 10, 2016, http://www.kidsinthe house.com/teenager/sexuality/transgender/when-parents-dont-support-their-transgendered-child?qt-more_videos=1#qt-more_videos.

CHAPTER 9

1. Peterson Toscano, "Transfigurations," Peterson Toscano, accessed February 13, 2016, https://petersontoscano.com/portfolio/transfigurations.

2. The first translation of the Bible to use the term "homosexual" was the 1946 edition of the Revised Standard Version. Prior to the publication of that translation, the word "homosexual" was never found in any Bible. For more information about the etymology of the word "homosexual," see Rev. Justin Cannon, "The Bible, Christianity, and Homosexuality," http://www.gaychurch.org/homosexuality-and-the-bible/the-bible-christianity-and-homosexuality/.

3. According to E. W. G. Masterman, mandrake plants "are still used in folklore medicine in Israel. The plant was well known as an aphrodisiac by the ancients (Song 7:13)." See James Orr, M.A., D.D., general editor, "Definition for 'MANDRAKES,'" *International Standard Bible Encyclopedia,* accessed March 24, 2016, http://www.bible-history.com/isbe/M/ MANDRAKES.

4. Greg Drinkwater, "Parashat Vayeshev—Joseph's Fabulous Technicolor Dreamcoat," Torah Queeries, December 16, 2006, accessed February 3, 2015, http://www.keshetonline.org/resource/josephs-fabulous-technicolor -dreamcoat-parashat-vayeshev/.

5. Ibid.

6. To find other biblical scholars who have interpreted Joseph's story through a gender nonconforming lens, simply Google the words "*ketonet passim* transgender."

7. Peterson Toscano, e-mail message to author, May 6, 2016.

8. "How Long Was Joseph In Potiphar's House? How Long In Prison?" Amazing Bible Timeline with World History, accessed March 25, 2016, http://amazingbibletimeline.com/bible_questions/q27_joseph _how_long_in_prison.

9. Cristen Conger, "Why did ancient Egyptian men wear cosmetics?" How Stuff Works, April 28, 2009, accessed April 8, 2016, http://history.howstuffworks.com/history-vs-myth/ancient-egyptian-cosmetics.htm.